LET ME EXPLAIN

When the end of his life work drew near, Teilhard de Chardin became anxious to draft the outline of what he considered the stages, the directions and the major elements of his thought. In a short paper dated May 1948 he drew up his outline and gave it the title: 'My intellectual position'.

This outline has guided J.-P. Demoulin in his choice of the extracts brought together in this book. These extracts are intended to serve as an introduction to Teilhard's original thought, and will also be useful to those who need a book for teaching purposes, as well as to those who wish to study Teilhard in greater detail. The major problems of Teilhard's vision are dealt with: his method, the vision of the past, the phenomenon of man, the future of man, human energy (action, love, personalism), Omega Point, God, the phenomenon of religion, the Church, ethics, mysticism.

It may be said that here, for the first time, Teilhard sets forth and summarizes the whole of his thought. It is for this reason that a phrase which often recurs in Père Teilhard's writings has been chosen as the title of this book, a phrase which he used when he sought to throw light on his statements: Let me explain (*Je m'explique*).

Pierre Teilhard de Chardin

LET ME EXPLAIN

Texts selected and arranged by
JEAN-PIERRE DEMOULIN

Translated by René Hague
and others

COLLINS
FONTANA BOOKS

First published by Éditions du Seuil
under the title *Je m'explique* in 1966

First published in the English language
by William Collins Sons & Co Ltd, London,
and Harper & Row, Inc., New York, 1970

First issued in Fontana Books, 1974
Second Impression December 1974

© Éditions du Seuil, 1966
© in the English translation
William Collins Sons & Co Ltd, London,
and Harper & Row, Inc., New York, 1970

Printed in Great Britain
Collins Clear-Type Press
London and Glasgow

Contents

Abbreviations

A.E. (Oeuvres VII) *L'Activation de l'Énergie*
A.M. *The Appearance of Man*
F.M. *The Future of Man*
H.E. *Human Energy*
H.U. *Hymn of the Universe*
M.D. *Le Milieu Divin (The Divine Milieu)*
M.P.N. *Man's Place in Nature*
P.M. *The Phenomenon of Man*
S.C. *Science and Christ*
V.P. *The Vision of the Past*
W.T.W. *Writings in Time of War*

References to F.M., M.D. and P.M. are to both the hardback and the Fontana paperback editions, 1969, 1964 and 1965.

Preface

In a letter to one of his correspondents Père Teilhard de Chardin himself shows us the best standpoint from which to understand and take in the full extent of his thought.

This is the commanding position adopted by Dr Jean-Pierre Demoulin as the starting-point for following Père Teilhard's intellectual journey. In this book he gives us the fruits of his persevering researches and of his experience. He is our personal guide to the peak from which we can look out over the boundless horizon covered by Teilhard's survey: the peak upon which, at the end of his days, with 'the splendour' of the final vision held in his eyes, he was to compose his swan-song:

'Energy becoming transformed into Presence.

'And in consequence the possibility can be seen, opening up for Man, of not only believing and hoping but (something much more unexpected and valuable) of loving, co-extensively and co-organically with the whole past, the present and the future of a Universe that is in process of concentrating upon itself.

'It would seem that a single ray of such a light falling like a spark, no matter where, on the Noosphere, would be bound to produce an explosion of such violence that it would almost instantaneously set the face of the Earth ablaze and make it entirely new.

'How is it, then, that as I look around me, still dazzled by what I have seen, I find that I am almost the only person of my kind, the only one to have seen? And so, I cannot, when asked, quote a single writer, a single work, that gives a clearly expressed description of the wonderful "Diaphany" that has transfigured everything for me?'

Preface

We should be grateful to Dr Demoulin for helping us so effectively to enter into the synthesis in which we can discern the 'Diaphany' that illuminated Père Teilhard's last exile. A penetrating study has given him a masterly knowledge of the writings of this great thinker: and while this has made him eminently qualified to produce the present volume, it has also enabled him to make a valuable contribution to the activities of the Teilhard Association.

JEANNE-MARIE MORTIER

Introduction

'I'd like to read Teilhard, but I don't know where to begin.' That sort of remark must be familiar to anyone who admires Père Teilhard and accepts his teaching; and yet, for all his anxiety to share his sense of wonderment with others, he finds himself at a loss for an answer. What advice can one give a beginner? As an initial introduction, *The Phenomenon of Man* is not only often difficult reading for a person who has not a scientific turn of mind, but also rather lengthy. It seemed a good plan, accordingly, to compile a selection of comparatively short passages (confining ourselves to Père Teilhard's own words) that would give a complete panoramic view of his thought.[1]

What is offered here, accordingly, is a selection from the nine volumes of the *Oeuvres* that have already been published, and from such unpublished writings as seemed necessary to clarify certain points. The choice has been made from those passages that are the most significant and also, so far as possible, the clearest and most simple.[2]

[1] Not that it is suggested that one can embark on a study without the over-all picture that is indispensable for the understanding of so highly synthesized a system of thought. The present attempt is justified by the fact that no current publication contains a 'complete and authentic' summary of his intellectual position, 'in relation to the World and to God'. His own short *Comment je vois* (1948, to be included in volume XI of the *Oeuvres*) is, indeed, such a synthesis, but it is so concise and abstract as to seem altogether too difficult for our immediate purpose.

[2] In part one, we have drawn freely upon three lectures given by Teilhard in Peking, in which his language is particularly easy: *The Future of Man as seen by a palaeontologist* (1941, in *The Future of Man*), *Man's Place in the Universe* (1942, in *The Vision of the Past*), and *Life and the Planets* (1945, in *The Future of Man*).

In order to draw up a summary of Père Teilhard's thought, all one needs to do is to refer to a typed note[3] which he sent in May 1948 to a colleague at Namur. This was published later in *Les Études Philosophiques* under the title *La Pensée du Père Teilhard de Chardin par lui-même*.[4] Again, in his *Journal*,[5] he twice sets out the general plan of his thought:

1. Physics (the phenomenon of man).
2. Dialectics (Omega Point, Revelation, Christ-Omega).
3. Metaphysics (Creative Union, Incarnation, Redemption, Evil).
4. Mysticism (evolutionary Charity, the mysticism of the West).

Two other similar writings enable us to fill out the structure of this summary: *Esquisse d'une dialectique de l'Esprit*,[6] which is an admirably clear statement of Teilhard's apologetics, and *Un sommaire de ma perspective 'phénoménologique' du monde* (1954). Of this latter Père Teilhard wrote: 'With this I am enclosing (for the record) two pages that I've just written for Tresmontant (I've already sent them to him) – but which it would be well for you to keep by you, for I believe it's the briefest and clearest statement of my position that I've written.'[7]

Thus the plan of this book coincides with that of the 1948 typed note (*Ma position intellectuelle*):

[3] *Ma position intellectuelle* (answer to a questionnaire which remained unpublished. No. 275 in the Bibliography included in Claude Cuénot, *Teilhard de Chardin*, London, 1965).

[4] Vol. 10, Oct.–Nov. 1955.

[5] *Journal*, vol. 3, 1947. Quoted by Claude Cuénot in *Situation de Teilhard de Chardin* (*Bulletin de la Société industrielle de Mulhouse*, no. 712, 1963, III, pp. 10–11).

[6] 1946, *L'Activation de l'Énergie* (*Oeuvres*, VII), p. 147.

[7] Letter of 19 Jan. 1954, to Mlle Jeanne Mortier.

Phenomenology, Apologetics, Mysticism. The neglect of Metaphysics is not due to any lack of care or understanding. The pages of *Comment je vois* and the brief flashes of illumination to be found in his *Journal* are sufficient to indicate that Teilhard probably had the makings of a great metaphysician, but metaphysics is too specialized and often too abstract a discipline to be contained in a 'digest', however carefully and sympathetically it may be produced. The metaphysical contribution of Teilhard is dealt with in Madeleine Barthélemy-Madaule's indispensable *Bergson et Teilhard de Chardin*,[8] which she will be supplementing by further works, more limited in scope but fuller in treatment.

The passages taken from Teilhard's writings are printed in roman, but not in quotation marks, followed by the appropriate references. Extracts from *Ma position intellectuelle* appear, in bold type, at the beginning or end of each chapter, the whole text of that statement being given as a conclusion at the end of the book.

The *Sommaire de ma perspective 'phénoménologique' du monde* (1954) serves as the conclusion to Part I.

Such comments as seemed desirable for the sake of clarity are printed in smaller type, and in italics.

The epilogue consists of three autobiographical statements by Père Teilhard, together with one of his prayers. These emphasize his mission as an apostle of Christ in the Universe. The statements were written at three peak-periods of his life:

1918 (at the Front): *The Priest.*

1934 (at the height of his scientific career): *How I Believe.*

1955 (his spiritual testament, one month before his death): *Le Christique.*

8 Paris, Éditions du Seuil, 1963.

Finally, on my own behalf and on that of the Belgian *Centre*, I must express my deep gratitude to Mlle Jeanne Mortier, who inherited Père Teilhard's writings and is responsible for their publication. She has been most generous in authorizing reproduction and has constantly given us the support of her friendly and understanding co-operation. Many, I hope and trust, will thank her for making it possible for them to become familiar with Père Teilhard's work.

JEAN-PIERRE DEMOULIN

Note on Teilhard's Vocabulary

Before reading what follows, one may perhaps find it useful to have a more exact definition of certain notions that are particularly important for an understanding of Père Teilhard's thought.

The general notions of phenomenon, phenomenology, metaphysics, dialectic, and apologetics, of emergence and transcendence, are given by Père Teilhard special meanings which may be defined as follows:

Phenomenon: As the etymology suggests: *that which appears,* that is to say, *that part of itself which being makes manifest* either to our senses or to our introspective consciousness. Physical, biological, psychological and social facts are all phenomena in as much as they can be described. When Teilhard looks at man and even at the Christian 'fact' as phenomena, he is leaving aside for the time being the question of their underlying causes or, when appropriate, their supernatural causes. He is confining himself to observing them simply as they present themselves to him. Thus we shall find him speaking of the human phenomenon, the spiritual, social, Christian, phenomenon.

Phenomenology: The method that seeks to bring out the meaning or reason (*logos*) of phenomena, by describing them as accurately and completely as possible. In the Preface to *The Phenomenon of Man* Teilhard tells us what he has tried to do: 'I have tried to establish a coherent order between antecedents and consequents. I have tried ... to discover ... *an experimental law* of recurrence which would express their *successive appearance* in time.' Again, in the Foreword, he sums up his work as 'an attempt to see and make others see what happens to man, and what conclusions are forced upon us, when he is placed fairly and squarely within the framework of phenomenon and appearance'. Teilhard's originality lies in having sought to describe the *whole* phenomenon, excluding no part of it. (See below, Chap. 1, and the beginning of Chap. 3.)

Metaphysics: This word has had a great many meanings in philosophy. Normally it means 'the science of being as such and of its ultimate causes', or a method of arriving at it. Sometimes Teilhard gives it a more restricted meaning when he sees in metaphysics only a method of 'reconstructing deductively, that is to say, *a priori,* the system observed (by phenomenological inquiry), starting from certain general principles that are accepted as absolute.'

Dialectic: A reflective method, a dialogue or discussion between thought and itself (often assisted by dialogue with others), a process in which thought connects its operations and views, and links together its judgements. Teilhard sometimes uses it in its current sense of 'the art of rigorously constructing chains of reasoning directed towards an end' (cf. p. 38). More exactly, he uses the term 'dialectic' to designate a stage in the whole process of his thought: apologetics (cf. Introduction, p. 12). This 'dialectic of the spirit' is a reflection that advances by alternating upon the postulates of action, i.e. 'energetics'. (See Part 2, which sets out this 'dialectic' or 'apologetics', p. 77.)

Apologetics: Originally, that branch of theology whose purpose is to defend the Christian religion against attack. It now, as it did for Père Teilhard, involves a dialectical approach that seeks to demonstrate the probability and reasonableness of Christian faith. It is thus the rational instrument used by the Christian who is concerned with apostolic work. (See the treatment in Part 2.)

Emergence: The appearance, in the course of evolution, of new and unpredictable properties. From the point of view of phenomenology, it is a threshold; from that of metaphysics, a creation. Underlying emergence is the Teilhardian notion of 'creative transformation'.

Transcendence: A type of relationship in which one term constitutes the other, without being limited by it. The soul transcends the body; God transcends the World.

In his phenomenological vision of the World, Teilhard brought out a number of far-reaching key-ideas: some of these define certain phases of evolution, while others stem from the actual process.

Examples of some of the former are:

Atomism: A general tendency, found in the Universe, towards granulation: in other words, to appear, when analysed, as a multitude of 'grains'. Thus there is a multitude of atoms, of molecules, of grains of sand, of plants, of animals, and even of thoughts ('atomism of the spirit').

Monad: Human individuality, in so far as it is an element of a whole and can reflect the whole.

Biosphere (from *Bios*, life): The word was first used by the Austrian geologist Eduard Suess (1831–1914). Teilhard uses it to mean 'the layer of vitalized (living) substance that envelops the earth';

Noosphere (from *Noos*, mind): 'The terrestrial sphere of

17

thinking substance.' It is the thinking envelope woven around the earth, above the biosphere, and made up by the totality of mankind. Its reality is already existing, and its density is constantly increasing through the rise in the human population, its inter-relations, and its spiritual quality.

Among the latter ideas, which come under the general notion of a 'cosmic drift', i.e. a general movement of the Universe within the passage of time, we may note:

Cosmogenesis: The global phenomenon of the evolution of the Universe. More particularly, it is a concept that emphasizes the fact that the Universe is, and has been, in continual process of formation since the beginning of time: in this, it is opposed to the ancient and medieval concept of a static cosmos.

The whole of this general movement may be seen by man, more and more fundamentally, as:

Biogenesis (the genesis of life)
Anthropogenesis (the genesis of the human species)
Noogenesis (genesis of spirit)
Christogenesis (genesis of the total Christ, of the Pleroma)

This same evolutionary process may be broken up, within the passage of time, into a number of major stages (cf. p. 50):

Moleculization: The transition from atoms to large molecules that will make possible the appearance of life. (The chief phenomenon of Biogenesis.)

Cephalization: The evolutionary tendency of the nervous system and sense-organs to concentrate in the head: this is particularly marked in the evolution of the vertebrates.

Cerebration: In the course of time, the brain of the highest order of the mammals, the primates, becomes ever more elaborated and convoluted. (The chief phenomenon of anthropogenesis.)

Hominization: The critical point through which the evolution of cerebralization passes, associated with upright posture, to attain thinking Man. (The chief phenomenon of noogenesis.)

Planetization: The phenomenon in which the ever-increasing mass of mankind, contained on an inelastic planet, converges upon itself. (One of the aspects of Christogenesis.)

To explain, on the phenomenological plane, this vast movement of 'cosmic in-folding', Teilhard formulates a law that introduces coherence into the successive temporal phases of evolution: this he calls the law of recurrence.

Recurrence: A repetition that seems to reproduce an already manifested plan, and which combines a certain periodicity with, at the same time, something new.

Law of recurrence: The law by which, at each successive stage of evolution, a new plurality – atomism, in fact – is formed, which allows a higher synthesis.

Phylum: A fascicle, within the evolutionary process, made up of a very large quantity of morphological units, each one of which represents a line of descent.

A further physical notion, that of 'entropy', has great importance as a negative influence on the process of cosmogenesis:

Entropy: The quantity by which dissipation of energy may be measured. Teilhard uses it primarily in the sense of the general law of increasing entropy; in accordance with this law, energy is continually dissipated with the passage of time, ultimately reducing the Universe to a mean state of diffuse agitation, in which all exchange of useful energy ceases. 'Everything around us seems to be descending towards this death of matter; everything except life.' (V.P., p. 149.)

Mention should also be made of some notions derived from religious terminology. Three of the most important may be defined as follows:

Parousia: The manifestation of the presence of Christ in all things (cf. M.D., p. 151). It will mark the end of all time.

Pantheism: The theory that All, or the Whole, and God are identical.

Pleroma: The whole of creation in its union with Christ.

Part One

Phenomenology

1. Seeing

The purpose of this first chapter is to illustrate Teilhard's method. Its originality is well brought out in a long extract from the Foreword to The Phenomenon of Man, *which marks a turning-point in the history of twentieth-century thought.*

This work may be summed up as an attempt *to see* and *to make others see* what happens to man, and what conclusions are forced upon us, when he is placed fairly and squarely within the framework of phenomenon and appearance.

Why should we want to see, and why in particular should we single out man as our object?

Seeing. We might say that the whole of life lies in that verb. That, doubtless, is why the history of the living world can be summarized as the elaboration of ever more perfect eyes within a cosmos in which there is always something more to be seen. After all, do we not judge the perfection of an animal, or the supremacy of a thinking being, by the penetration and synthetic power of their gaze? To try to see more and better is not a matter of whim or curiosity or self-indulgence. *To see or to perish* is the very condition laid upon everything that is an element, by reason of the mysterious gift of existence. And this, at a higher level, is man's condition. (P.M., p. 31; Fontana, p. 35.)

If to see is really to become more, if vision is really fuller being, then we should look closely at man in order to increase our capacity to live.

But to do this we must focus our eyes correctly.

From the dawn of his existence, man has been held up as a spectacle to himself. Indeed for tens of centuries he has looked at nothing but himself. Yet he has only just begun to take a scientific view of his own significance in the physical world. There is no need to be surprised at this slow awakening. It often happens that what stares us in the face is the most difficult to perceive. The child has to learn to separate out the images which assail the newly-opened retina. For man to discover man and take his full measure, a whole series of 'senses' have been necessary, whose gradual acquisition, as we shall show, covers and punctuates the whole history of the struggles of the mind.

A sense of spatial immensity, in greatness and smallness, disarticulating and spacing out, within a sphere of indefinite radius, the orbits of the objects which press round us;

A sense of depth, pushing back laboriously through endless series and measureless distances of time, which a sort of gravitational force tends continually to condense for us in a thin layer of the past;

A sense of number, discovering and grasping unflinchingly the bewildering multitude of material or living elements involved in the slightest transformation of the universe;

A sense of proportion, realizing as best we can the difference of physical scale which separates, both in rhythm and dimension, the atom from the nebula, the infinitesimal from the immense;

A sense of quality, or of novelty, enabling us to distinguish in nature certain absolute stages of perfection and growth, without upsetting the physical unity of the world;

A sense of movement, capable of perceiving the irresistible developments hidden in extreme slowness – extreme agitation concealed beneath a veil of immobility – the entirely new insinuating itself into the heart of the monotonous repetition of the same things;

A sense, lastly, of the organic, discovering physical links and structural unity under the superficial juxtaposition of successions and collectivities.

Without these qualities to illuminate our vision, man will remain indefinitely for us – whatever is done to make us see – what he still represents to so many minds: an erratic object in a disjointed world. Conversely, we have only to rid our vision of the threefold illusion of smallness, plurality and immobility, for man effortlessly to take the central position we prophesied – the momentary summit of an anthropogenesis which is itself the crown of a cosmogenesis.

Man is unable to see himself entirely unrelated to mankind, neither is he able to see mankind unrelated to life, nor life unrelated to the universe. (P.M., pp. 33–4; Fontana, pp. 37–8.)

Such a vision will therefore be scientific in the broad sense of the word. It will distinguish the pattern into which facts (phenomena) fall and their succession, and, as every science does, it will look for hypotheses that give coherence to the pattern.

Discussing scientific views as a scientist, I must and shall stick strictly to the examination and arrangement of what is perceptible, that is to say of 'phenomena'. Being concerned with the links and order of succession revealed by these phenomena, I shall not deal with their deep causality. (V.P., p. 217.)

[I am dealing] with man *solely* as a phenomenon; but . . . also with the *whole* phenomenon of man (P.M., p. 29; Fontana, p. 31.)

My only aim, and my only vantage-ground in these pages, is to try to see; that is to say, to try to develop a *homogeneous* and *coherent* perspective of our general experience extended to man. (P.M., p. 35; Fontana, p. 39.)

Père Teilhard begins the summary of his thought (1948) as follows:

'In its essence, the thought of Père Teilhard de Chardin is expressed not in a metaphysics but in a sort of phenomenology.'

2. The Vision of the Past

This second chapter will be an attempt to show that the study of the earth's past is sufficient in itself to oblige us to accept not only the idea of evolution but a clear pattern of a rise of consciousness throughout the ages: an ascent of which man now represents the culminating point.

But if we are to make this journey into the past, we must allow ourselves to be permeated by this 'sense of depth', referred to earlier, so that we may discover the new real dimension of things which the discovery of time obliges us to accept.

I. THE DISCOVERY OF TIME

To understand the spiritual events which are so convulsing the age we live in we need to be constantly looking back (I shall repeat this) to their common origin – the discovery of Time.

This does not mean that men had to wait till the nineteenth century before seeing how events, grouped in long series, were absorbed into the past. They talked of Time long before our day, and even measured it, so far as their instruments permitted, as we do now. But Time remained for them a homogeneous quantity, capable of being divided into parts. The course of centuries lying ahead and behind us could be conceived of in theory as abruptly stopping or beginning at a given moment, the real and total duration of the Universe being supposed not to exceed a few thousand years. On the other hand, it appeared that within those few millennia any object could be arbitrarily displaced and removed to another point without undergoing any change in its environment or in itself. Socrates could have been born in the place of Descartes, and vice versa. Temporally (no less than spatially) human beings were regarded as interchangeable.

This, broadly, is what was accepted by the greatest minds up to and including Pascal.

But since then, under the influence, unconcerted but convergent, of the natural, historical and physical sciences, an entirely new concept has almost imperceptibly shaped itself in our minds.

We have in the first place realized that every constituent element of the world (whether a being or a phenomenon) has of necessity emerged from that which preceded it – so much so that it is as physically impossible for us to conceive of a thing in Time without 'something before it' as it would be to imagine the same thing in Space without 'something beside it'. In this sense every particle of reality, instead of constituting an approximate point in itself, extends from the previous fragment to the next in an indivisible thread running back into infinity.

Secondly we have found that the threads or chains of elements thus formed are not homogeneous over their extent, but that each represents a naturally ordered series in which the links can no more be exchanged than can the successive states of infancy, adolescence, maturity and senility in our own lives.

Finally, we have gradually come to understand that no elemental thread in the Universe is wholly independent in its growth of its neighbouring threads. Each forms part of a sheaf; and the sheaf in turn represents a higher order of thread in a still larger sheaf – and so on indefinitely.

This is the organic whole of which today we find ourselves to be a part, without being able to escape from it. Whereas for the last two centuries our study of science, history and philosophy has appeared to be a matter of speculation, imagination and hypothesis, we can now see that in fact, in countless subtle ways, the concept of Evolution has been weaving its web around us. We believed that we did not change; but now, like newborn infants whose eyes are opening to the light, we are becoming aware of a world in which neo-Time is endowing the totality of our knowledge and beliefs with a new structure and a new direction. (F.M., pp. 83–5; Fontana, pp. 86–8.)

For our age, to have become conscious of evolution means something very different from and much more than having discovered one further fact, however massive and important that fact may be. It means (as happens with a child when he acquires the sense of perspective) that we have become alive to a new *dimension*. The idea of evolution: not, as is sometimes still said, a mere hypothesis, but a condition of all experience – or again, if you prefer the expression, the universal curve to which all our present and future ways of constructing the universe must conform, if they are to be scientifically valid or even thinkable. (S.C., p. 193.)

This is something we must understand once and for all: for us and for our descendants, there is henceforth a final and permanent change in psychological times and dimensions. (A.E. (*Oeuvres* VII), p. 264.)

II. THE RISE OF CONSCIOUSNESS

The meticulous work accomplished in the past hundred years by the collectors of fossils, the results of which they have patiently recorded in innumerable papers and in barbarous language, perfectly incomprehensible to non-initiates, the paraphernalia of systematics and the clutter on the museum shelves, all this has made a contribution of the utmost importance to the World's thinking. It has added to the sum of human knowledge an item of extraordinary interest – *a segment of the past extending over some three hundred million years.* (F.M., p. 63; Fontana, p. 66.)

'When observed through a sufficient depth of time (*millions* of years) Life can be seen to move. Not only does it move but it advances in a definite direction. And not only does it advance, but in observing its progress we can discern the process or practical mechanism whereby it does so.'

These are three propositions which may be briefly developed as follows:

a. *Life moves.* This calls for no demonstration. Everyone in these days knows how greatly all living forms have changed if we compare two moments in the earth's history sufficiently separated in time. In any period of ten million years Life practically grows a new skin.

b. *In a definite direction.* This is the crucial point which has to be clearly understood. While accepting the undeniable fact of a general transformation of Life in the course of time, many biologists still maintain that this takes place without following any defined course, in any direction and at random. This contention, disastrous to any idea of progress, is refuted, in my view, by the tremendous fact of the continuing 'cerebralization' of living creatures. Research shows that from the lowest to the highest level of the organic world there is a persistent and clearly defined thrust of animal forms towards species with more sensitive and elaborate nervous systems. A growing 'innervation' and 'cephalization' of organisms: the working of this law is visible in every living group known to us, the smallest no less than the largest. We can follow it in insects as in vertebrates; and among the vertebrates we can follow it from class to class, from order to order, and from family to family. There is an amphibian phase of the brain, a reptilian phase, a mammalian phase. In the mammals we see the brain grow as time passes and become more complex among the ungulates, the carnivores and above all the primates. So much so that one could draw a steadily rising Curve of Life taking Time as one co-ordinate and, as the other, the quantity (and quality) of nervous tissue existing on earth at each geological stage.

What else can this mean except that, as shown by the development of nervous systems, there is a continual heightening, a rising tide of consciousness which visibly manifests itself on our planet in the course of the ages?

c. We come to the third point. What is the *underlying process* whose existence we can perceive in this continual heightening of consciousness, as revealed by the organic evolution of the nervous system and the brain? Let us look more closely in the light of the latest data supplied by the combined ingenuity of an army of research workers. As we are beginning to realize, there are probably tens of thousands of atoms grouped in a single virus molecule. There are certainly tens of thousands of molecules grouped in a single cell. There are millions of cells in a single brain. There are millions of brains in a single ant-hill. . . .

What does this atomism signify except that the stuff of the Cosmos, governed at its lower end (as we already knew) by forces of dispersal which slowly cause it to dissolve into atoms, now shows itself to be subjected, at the other end, to an extraordinary power of enforced coalescence, of which the outcome is the emergence, in step with this, of an ever-increasing amount of spiritual energy in matter that is ever more powerfully synthesized? Let me note that there is nothing metaphysical in this. I am not seeking to define either Spirit or Matter. I am simply saying, without leaving the physical field, that the greatest discovery made in this century is probably the realization that the passage of Time may best be measured by the gradual gathering of Matter in superposed groups, of which the arrangement, ever richer and more centred, is surrounded by an ever more luminous fringe of liberty and interiority. The phenomenon of growing consciousness on earth, in short, is directly due to the increasingly advanced organization of more and more complicated elements, successively created by the working of chemistry and of Life. At the present time I can see no more satisfactory solution of the enigma presented to us by the physical progress of the Universe. (F. M., pp. 64–6; Fontana, pp. 67–9.)

III. THE PLACE OF MAN IN THE FOREFRONT OF LIFE

In what I have said thus far I have been looking at Life in general, in its entirety. We come now to the particular case which interests us most – the problem of Man.

The existence of an ascendant movement in the Universe has been revealed to us by the study of palaeontology. Where is Man to be situated in this line of progress?

The answer is clear. If, as I maintain, the movement of the cosmos towards the highest degree of consciousness is not an optical illusion, but represents the essence of biological evolution, then, in the curve traced by Life, Man is unquestionably situated at the topmost point; and it is he, by his emergence and existence, who finally proves the reality of the trajectory and defines it – 'the dot on the i'. . . .

Indeed, within the field accessible to our experience, does not the birth of Thought stand out as a critical point through which all the striving of previous ages passes and is consummated – the critical point traversed by consciousness, when, by force of concentration, it ends by reflecting upon itself? (F.M., p. 67; Fontana, p. 70.)

This critical point of 'reflection' will be defined more exactly at the beginning of the next chapter: 'What is the Phenomenon of Man?'

The fundamental line of growth – one becomes progressively less able to avoid this almost direct evidence – is the advance of organic beings towards an increase of spontaneity and consciousness. The kind of peak – it would be childish to deny this out of fear of some kind of 'anthropomorphism' – is, at this present moment, man. Man, no doubt, can be defined on the non-relief map of systematics as a family of primates recognizable by certain details of skull, pelvis and limbs. But if we wish to place him in a truly natural picture of the world, which takes into account the whole evolution of life, his principal definition must be made by his property of 'taking the lead' at this moment in the movement drawing organic beings towards greater possibilities of knowledge and action. Similarly, before man's arrival, the entire line of higher primates already occupied a place apart in nature. But man, by his arrival, swept them aside, making so decisive an advance over everything around him that he is now alone in the lead. (V.P., pp. 165–6.)

3. The Phenomenon of Man

The Vision of the Past has enabled us to appreciate the general current of Evolution and to set the 'human zoological group' at the head of that movement.

We may now examine more closely the fundamental law of this cosmic evolution, which makes it coherent for us.

The best vantage-point we can choose for this is that at which the whole process of Evolution is clearly illuminated: the only point, too, at which we are, by nature, at home. We turn, therefore, to the study of 'the phenomenon of man'.

I. WHAT IS THE PHENOMENON OF MAN?

By the expression 'the Phenomenon of Man' we mean here the empirical fact of the appearance in our universe of the power of reflection and thought. For enormous periods the earth certainly lacked any real manifestation of life. Then for another enormous period in the layer of organic matter which appeared on its solid or watery envelope, it presented only signs of spontaneity, and unreflective consciousness (the animal feels and perceives; but he does not appear to know that he feels and perceives). Finally, in a relatively recent epoch, spontaneity and consciousness acquired on earth, in the zone of life that had become human, the property of isolating and individualizing themselves in their own right. Man knows that he knows. He emerges from his actions. He dominates them in however feeble a way. He can therefore abstract, combine and foresee. He reflects. He thinks. (V.P., p. 161.)

From our empirical point of view, reflection is, as the

34

word indicates, the power acquired by a consciousness to turn in upon itself, to take possession of itself *as of an object* endowed with its own particular consistence and value: no longer merely to know oneself; no longer merely to know, but to know that one knows. By this individualization of himself in the depths of himself, the living element, which heretofore has been spread out and divided over a diffuse circle of perceptions and activities, is constituted for the first time as a *centre* in the form of a point at which all impressions and experiences knit themselves together and fuse into a unity that is conscious of its own organization.

Now the consequences of such a transformation are immense, visible as clearly in nature as any of the facts recorded in physics or astronomy. The being who is the object of his own reflection, in consequence of that very doubling back upon himself, becomes in a flash able to raise himself into a new sphere. In reality, another world is born. Abstraction, logic, reasoned choice and inventions, mathematics, art, calculation of space and time, anxieties and dreams of love – all these activities of *inner life* are nothing else than the effervescence of the newly-formed centre as it explodes upon itself.

Proceeding from that, I have a question to ask. If, as follows from the foregoing, it is the fact of being 'reflective' which constitutes the strictly 'intelligent' being, can we seriously doubt that intelligence is the evolutionary lot proper to man and to man *only*? If not, can we, under the influence of some false modesty, hesitate to admit that man's possession of it constitutes a radical advance on all forms of life that have gone before him? Admittedly the animal knows. *But it cannot know that it knows:* that is quite certain. If it could, it would long ago have multiplied its inventions and developed a system of internal constructions that could not have escaped our observation. In consequence it is denied access to a whole domain of reality in which we can move freely. We are separated by a chasm – or a threshold – which it cannot cross. Because we are reflective we are not only different but quite other. It is not merely a matter of change of degree, but of a change of nature, resulting from a change of state. (P.M., pp. 165–6; Fontana, pp. 183–4.)

This event can serve as a point of departure for many philosophical, moral, or religious trains of thought. We would only view it here, at least preliminarily, simply from the historical and scientific point of view. For a very long time there was no thought on earth. Now there is, and to such a degree, that the face of things is entirely changed. Now we are really viewing a purely scientific fact, a phenomenon. What are we to think of this phenomenon?

It is an extraordinary thing. Scientists, for the last hundred years have been examining with unheard-of subtlety and daring, the mysteries of material atoms and the living cell. They have weighed the electron and the stars. They have divided the vegetable and animal kingdom into hundreds of thousands of species. They are striving with infinite patience to link the human form anatomically to that of the other vertebrates. Passing more directly to the study of our zoological type, they endeavour to examine the springs of human psychology, or to isolate the laws governing the exchanges of products and services in the growing complexity of our society. Now in the midst of these great labours, almost nobody has yet decided to put the main question: 'But what exactly is the phenomenon of man?' That is to say, in rather more precise terms, 'What is the place and purpose of this extraordinary power of thought in the development of the world of experience?' Let us repeat: Man today is scientifically known and recognized by a great number of detailed properties or connections. But, perhaps because some are afraid of lapsing into metaphysics and others of desecrating the 'soul' by treating it as a simple physical object, man, in his special and most revealing characteristics, that is to say in what are called his 'spiritual' properties, is still left out of our general pictures of the world. Hence this paradoxical fact: there is a science of the universe without man, and there is also a science of man as marginal to the universe; but there is not yet a science of the universe that embraces man as such. Present-day physics (taking this word in the broad Greek sense of 'a systematic understanding of all nature') does not yet give a place to thought; which means that it still exists in complete independence of the most remarkable phenomenon exposed by nature to our observation. (V.P., pp. 161–2.)

The three characteristics which make the human individual a truly unique object in the eyes of Science, once we have made up our minds to regard man not merely as a chance arrival but as an integral element of the physical world, are as follows:

a. An extreme physico-chemical complexity (particularly apparent in the brain) which permits us to consider him the most highly synthesized form of matter known to us in the Universe;

b. Arising out of this, an extreme degree of organization which makes him the most perfectly and deeply centred of all cosmic particles within the field of our experience;

c. Finally, and correlative with the above, the high degree of psychic development (reflection, thought) which places him head and shoulders above all other conscious beings known to us. (F.M., p. 87; Fontana, p. 90.)

We must accept what science tells us, that man was born from the earth. But, more logical than the scientists who lecture us, we must carry this lesson to its conclusion: that is to say, accept that man was born entirely from the world – not only his flesh and bones but his incredible power of thought. Let us consider him, without reducing his stature, as a phenomenon. (H.E., p. 20.)

To establish the value of this new viewpoint . . . my only form of argument will be that universally employed by modern science, that and that alone: by which I mean the argument of 'coherence'. In a world whose single business seems to be to organize itself in relation to itself, that is by definition the more *true*, which better harmonizes in relation to ourselves a larger body of facts. (H.E., p. 94.)

II. THE NOTION OF COMPLEXITY

We will define the 'complexity' of a thing as the quality the thing possesses of being composed –

    a. of a larger number of elements, which are

    b. more tightly organized among themselves.

In this sense an atom is more complex than an electron, a molecule more complex than an atom, and a living cell more complex than the highest chemical nuclei of which it is composed, the difference depending (on this I insist) not only on the number and diversity of the elements included in each case, but at least as much on the number and correlative variety of the links formed between these elements. It is not, therefore, a matter of *simple* multiplicity but of organized multiplicity; not simple complication but *centred* complication.

This idea of complexity (more exactly, centro-complexity)

is easily grasped. In a universe where science ends by analysing everything and taking everything apart, it simply expresses a characteristic proper to each kind of body, like its mass, volume or any other dimension. . . .

The coefficient of complexity enables us to establish among the natural units which it has helped us to 'identify' and isolate, a system of classification that is no less natural and universal. Let us try to depict this classification in schematic form, as it might be drawn on a blackboard.

At the very bottom of the board we have the ninety-two simple chemical elements (from hydrogen to uranium) formed by groups of atomic nuclei together with their electrons.

Above these come the molecules composed of groups of atoms. These molecules, in the case of the carbon compounds, may become enormous. In the albuminoids (or proteins) there may be thousands of associated atoms: the molecular weight of haemoglobin is 68,000.

Above these again come the mysterious viruses, strange bodies producing a variety of maladies in animals and plants, concerning which we do not yet know if they are monstrous chemical molecules or living infra-bacteria. Their molecular weight runs into millions.

Higher still we come to the lowest cells. I do not know if any attempt has yet been made to ascertain the atomic content of these (it must be billions) but they are undoubtedly groups of proteins.

And finally we reach the world of higher living forms, each composed of groups of cells. To take a very simple instance, that of the plant duckweed; its content is estimated to be 4×10^{20} atoms.

This scheme of classification, based essentially on the

intimate structure of beings, is undeniably *natural* in principle.

Moreover, when arranged according to our scale of complexity, the elements succeed one another *in the historical order of their birth*. The place in the scale occupied by each corpuscle situates the element chronologically in the genesis of the Universe, that is to say, in Time. It dates it.

Thus the rising scale conforms both to the ascending movement towards higher consciousness and to the unfolding of evolutionary time. Does not this suggest that, by using the degree of complexity as a guide, we may advance very much more surely than by following any other lead as we seek to penetrate to the truth of the world and to assess, in terms of absolute values, the relative importance, the place, of all things? (F.M., pp. 105–7; Fontana, pp. 109–12.)

III. A THIRD INFINITE, OR, THE INFINITELY COMPLEX

Physics has so far been built up from a consideration of a single one of the world's axes: the axis that rises up, through intermediate magnitudes (in which we are physically included), from the extremely small to the extremely large, from the infinitesimal to the immense. Physics is still concerned with only two infinites. Now, this is not enough. If I am, scientifically, to cover the whole of my experience, I must have in my mind and allow for in the Universe a further 'infinite', as real as the other two: by this I mean the infinite of complexity. The bodies we see around us are not simply small and large. They are also simple or complex.

Moreover, the distance (estimating it numerically – and very approximately – simply by the number of elements combined) from the extreme of complexity in the particles we know is just as astronomical as that between stellar and atomic magnitudes. It is, therefore, in a strictly literal sense, and by no means metaphorically, that we may speak in science of a 'third infinite', which, starting from the infinitesimal, builds itself up in the immense to the level of the median: and that, let me repeat, is the infinity of complexity.

When we introduce into our fundamental plan of the Universe this axis of complexities, it is not simply the result of trying to cover more explicitly and accurately a wider section of the world of experience. The most interesting consequence of the transformation we effect is that the phenomena of life (consciousness, freedom, invention) are thereby readily linked to the phenomena of matter. In other words, biology is quite naturally incorporated into physics. If in fact, as universal experience shows us, life represents a controlled whole of properties that appear and develop as a function of the increasing physico-chemical complexity of organized material groups, then surely we must lay down a further principle. It is one that is completely consonant with another fact, now universally accepted, that every infinite is characterized by certain effects that are strictly proper to it alone. The principle I mean is that consciousness is the peculiar and specific property of *organized states* of matter; it is a property that is hardly perceptible, and therefore negligible, when we are dealing with low values of complexity, but it gradually makes itself felt and finally becomes dominant when we reach high values. . . . On the one hand we have physics, in the strict sense of the word, which is chiefly concerned to bring out the statistical pattern of very simple elements (which accordingly enjoy an infinitely small degree of life): taking these elements in very large numbers, from the infinitesimal to the immense. On the other hand, we have biology: it branches off in a different but allied direction from physics and confines itself to the median, studying the behaviour and association of particles that are extremely complex and therefore appreciably interiorized, each particle being capable of being treated in isolation. Thus these two sciences, the science of matter and the science of life, are not opposed but complementary to one another. (*Comment je vois*, 1948, paras. 1–2.)

IV. A LAW OF RECURRENCE: THE LAW OF COMPLEXITY–CONSCIOUSNESS

However wide the distinction in nature we still, for philosophical reasons, think it necessary to draw between life and matter, there comes to light in the order of phenomena a law of recurrence which is found by experience to link together the appearance of the two. (F.M., p. 107; Fontana, p. 111.)

Everyone has known from the beginning that organized matter is endowed with spontaneity in combination with psychic inwardness. Everyone also knows today that this organic matter is amazingly complicated. Why, in the light of the great discoveries of modern physics, should we not state quite simply that two and two make four? In other words, transforming the problem into a solution, why not say this: 'Absolutely inert and totally brute matter *does not exist*. Every element of the Universe contains, at least to an infinitesimal degree, some germ of inwardness and spontaneity, that is to say of consciousness. In extremely simple and extremely numerous corpuscles (which only manifest themselves by their statistical effects) this property remains imperceptible to us, *as if it did not exist*. On the other hand its importance grows with its complexity – or, which comes to the same thing, with the degree of "centration" of the corpuscles on themselves. From an atomic complexity of the order of millions (virus) onwards, it begins to come into our experience. In the higher reaches it shows itself in successive leaps (in a series of psychic "quanta"). Finally in man, after the critical point of "reflection", it takes the form of thought and thereafter becomes dominant. Just as in the infinitely small, great numbers explain the determinism of physical laws; and just as in immensity, the curvature of space explains the forces of gravity, so, in the third infinity, complexity (and the "centredness" resulting from it) gives rise to the phenomena of freedom.'

Thus everything in the universe around us surely becomes clearer.

And the stars? you will ask. And the galaxies? You have said nothing about them. What place do they have in this story?

Despite their corpuscular appearance, the stars certainly do not form a natural prolongation of the line of atoms. This, as we have just seen, culminates in life in the middle zone of the world. The stars, on the other hand, repeat this line symmetrically on the side of the very great. The stars, one might say, are the laboratories, the place of generation, the 'matrix' of atoms. The larger a star is, the simpler is its constitution. Inversely, the smaller and colder (up to a certain optimum) a sidereal body is, the larger the range of its elements grows, and the more these elements build up into complex edifices. Such is the case of the earth, the only known star on which we can follow the higher phases of this development. From this point of view the appearance of life takes the form of a conjoint effect of 'galactic gas' and 'electronic gas', reacting on one another in the middle dimensions. (V.P., pp. 225–6.)

Life is apparently nothing but the privileged exaggeration of a fundamental cosmic tendency (as fundamental as entropy or gravitation) which may be called the 'Law of complexity-consciousness', and which can be expressed as follows:

'Left long enough to itself, under the prolonged and universal play of chance, matter manifests the property of arranging itself in more and more complex groupings, and at the same time in ever-deepening layers of consciousness; this double and combined movement of physical infolding and psychic interiorization once started, continuing, accelerating, and growing to its utmost extent.' (A.M., p. 139.)

V. CONSEQUENCES: MAN'S PLACE IN THE UNIVERSE

In science (and elsewhere) the great test of truth is coherence and fruitfulness. For our minds, the more order a theory imposes on our vision of the world, and, at the same time, the more capable it shows itself of directing and sustaining the forward movement of our powers of research and construction, the more certain that theory is. (*True theory* = *the most profitable.*)

With this understanding, let us take up our position (at least provisionally and hypothetically) in the universe with three infinites which I have just postulated. Let us act as if this universe were the *true one*, and try to see what takes place.

A long series of corollaries immediately appears: and the

closely linked chain of them leads us much further than you would think towards the harmonization of our knowledge and the guiding of our actions.

a. *The significance of consciousness*

In the first place a natural connection is drawn between the two worlds of physics and psychology, hitherto supposed irreconcilable. Matter and consciousness are bound together: not in the sense that consciousness becomes directly measurable, but in the sense that it becomes organically and physically rooted in the same cosmic process with which physics is concerned.[1]

In the second place, and by the same fact, the appearance of consciousness ceases to be a chance, strange, aberrant, fortuitous occurrence in the universe. It becomes on the contrary a regular and general phenomenon connected with the global drift of cosmic matter towards increasingly high molecular groupings. Life appears wherever it becomes possible in the universe.

In the third place, the phenomenon 'consciousness', by the very fact that it is recognized to be general, tends to present itself as essential and fundamental. Not only *a* physical phenomenon, but *the* phenomenon. We have already known for some years that towards the bottom matter tends to vanish by disaggregation of atomic nuclei. And here is life, showing itself as symmetrically the exactly opposite process: a corpuscular aggregation. On the one hand, a fall of great numbers towards states of greatest probability. On the other a persistent, incredible but undeniable rise towards the smallest numbers by way of improbability. The movements

[1] The reference is to the law of recurrence examined above.

are of the same universal vastness. But while the former destroys, the latter constructs. Must it not then be this latter rise of consciousness that represents the true course of our universe through time: the very axis of cosmogenesis?

b. *The significance of man*

And hence (fourth corollary) the significance of man is growing, and his place is becoming scientifically more precise.

On the curve of moleculization, as we have just drawn it, man is clearly not the first in size. By the quantity of corpuscles assembled in his body (by his total number of molecules) he clearly stands below the elephant or the whale: But on the other hand, it is certainly in him, in the thousands of millions of cells of his brain, that matter has now reached its maximum of linked complication and centralized organization. Chronologically and structurally, man is indubitably in the field of our experience, the last formed, the most highly complex and at the same time the most deeply centred of all the 'molecules'.

There are still certain physicists who scoff at 'man's pretensions to give himself an inexplicable superiority in the world'. I am certain that a generation hence, the attitude accepted by scientists will be that of Julian Huxley when he declared that man is the highest, the richest, the most significant object within range of our investigations, because it is in him that cosmic evolution is culminating at this moment before our eyes, having become, by our reflection, conscious of itself.

The old anthropocentrism was wrong in imagining man to be the geometrical and necessary juridical centre of a static universe. But its anticipations are verified in a manner at once higher and more humble, now that man (who was once believed to be engulfed in a universe immensely extended by physics) justifiably reappears at the very forefront of the wave of moleculization which carries the world forward.

Everything falls into place, everything takes shape, from the lowest to the highest, in the present and the past of a universe in which a generalized physics succeeds in embracing without confusing the phenomena of radiation and the spiritual phenomenon. *Coherence.*

And, in addition, everything is illumined (though in a diffuse manner, as is right) in the direction of the future. *Fruitfulness.*

c. *Fruitfulness for human action*

I wish to insist on this decisive point before concluding.

One evident characteristic of the curve of moleculization, as drawn, is that it is not closed, not stopped. At present it ends with man. But dare we think that it can and should extend further? And how? Man is momentarily a *climax* in the universe; and a leading shoot also, to the extent that by his intense psychism he confirms the reality and fixes the direction of a rise of consciousness through things. But may he not also be the *bud* from which something more complicated and more centred than man himself is to emerge?

In man, up to now, we have only considered the individual edifice; the body with its thousand billion cells, and above all the brain, with its thousand millions of nervous nuclei. But while man is an individual centred in himself (that is to say a 'person') does he not at the same time stand as an *element* in relation to some new and higher synthesis? We know atoms as sums of nuclei and electrons; molecules as sums of atoms; cells as collections of molecules. Could there not be, in formation ahead of us, a humanity which will be the sum of organized persons? And is not this, moreover, the only logical manner of extending, *by recurrence* (in the direction of greater centred complexity and greater consciousness), the curve of universal moleculization?

Here is the idea, long dreamt of by sociology, reappearing today, this time with a scientific foundation, in the books of professional scientists (Haldane, Huxley, Sherrington and so many others). Fantastic, you may think. But must not everything be fantastic if it is not to be false, in the direction of the three infinites? (V.P., pp. 227-9.)

VI. SUMMARY

A certain law of recurrence, underlying and dominating all experience, forces itself on our attention. It is the law of complexity-consciousness, by which, within life, the stuff of the cosmos folds in upon itself continually more closely, following a process of organization whose measure is a corresponding increase of tension (or psychic t°).

In the field of our observation, reflective man represents the highest term attained by an element in this process of organization.

4. The Future of Man

Above individual man, however, this involution is carried further, in mankind, by the social phenomenon, at the term of which can be discerned a higher critical point of collective reflection. From this point of view 'hominization' (including socialization) is a convergent phenomenon: in other words it displays an upper limit or point of internal maturity.

1. SOCIALIZATION: FORMATION OF THE NOOSPHERE

The first thing to give us pause, as we survey the progress of human collectivization, is what I would call the inexorable nature of a phenomenon which arises directly and automatically out of the conjunction of two factors, both of a structural kind: first, the confined surface of the globe, and secondly, the incessant multiplication, within this restricted space, of human units endowed by ever improving means of communication with a rapidly increasing scope for action; to which may be added the fact that their advanced psychic development makes them pre-eminently capable of influencing and inter-penetrating one another. Under the combined effect of these two natural pressures a sort of mass-concretion of mankind upon itself comes of necessity into operation.

But, the second noteworthy point, this phenomenon of solidifying, or cementing, turns out to be no sudden or unpredictable event. Looking at the picture as a whole we see that Life, from its lowest level, has never been able to effect its syntheses except through the progressively closer association of its elements, whether in the oceans or on land. Upon an imaginary earth of constantly increasing extent, living organisms, being only loosely associated, might well have remained at the monocellular stage (if indeed they had ever got so far); and certainly man, if free to live in a scattered state, would never have reached even the neolithic stage of social development. The totalization in progress in the modern world is in fact nothing but the natural climax and paroxysm of a process of grouping which is fundamental to the elaboration of organized matter. Matter does not vitalize or super-vitalize itself except by compression.

I do not think it is possible to reflect upon this twofold inrooting, both structural and evolutionary, which characterizes the social events affecting us, without being at first led to the surmise, and finally overwhelmed by the evidence, that the collectivization of the human race, at present accelerated, is nothing other than a higher form adopted by the process of moleculization on the surface of our planet. The first phase was the formation of proteins up to the stage of the cell. In the second phase individual cellular complexes were formed, up to and including man. We are now at the beginning of a third phase, the formation of an organico-social super-complex, which, as may easily be demonstrated, *can only occur in the case of reflective, personalized elements.* First the vitalization of matter, associated with the grouping of molecules; then the hominization of Life, associated with a super-grouping of cells; and finally the *planetization* of Mankind, associated with a *closed* grouping of people: Mankind, born on this planet and spread over its entire surface, coming gradually to form around its earthly matrix a single, major organic unity, *enclosed upon itself;* a single, hyper-complex, hyper-centred, hyper-conscious arch-molecule, co-extensive with the heavenly body on which it was born. Is not this what is happening at the present time – the closing of this spherical, thinking circuit? (F.M., pp. 114–15; Fontana, pp. 118–20.) – the growth, outside and above the biosphere, of an added planetary layer, an envelope of thinking substance, to which, for the sake of convenience and symmetry, I have given the name of Noosphere. (F.M., p. 157; Fontana, p. 163.)

II. THE NOOSPHERE: VERIFICATION OF A HYPOTHESIS

Clearly this is a matter in which I cannot compel your assent. But I can assure you, of my own experience, that the acceptance of this organic and realistic view of the social phenomenon is both eminently satisfying to our reason and fortifying to our will. (*Coherence and fruitfulness.*)

a. *Satisfying to the intelligence above all.* For if it be true that at this moment mankind is embarking upon what I have called its 'phase of planetization', then everything is clarified, everything in our field of vision acquires a new sharpness of outline.

The tightening network of economic and psychic bonds in which we live and from which we suffer, the growing compulsion to act, to produce, to think collectively which so disquiets us – what do they become, seen in this way, except the first portents of the super-organism which, woven of the threads of individual men, is preparing (theory and fact are at one on this point) not to mechanize and submerge us, but to raise us, by way of increasing complexity, to a higher awareness of our own personality?

The increasing degree, intangible, and too little noted, in

which present-day thought and activity are influenced by the passion for discovery; the progressive replacement of the workshop by the laboratory, of production by research, of the desire for well-being by the desire for *more*-being – what do these things betoken if not the growth in our souls of a great impulse towards super-evolution?

The profound cleavage in every kind of social group (families, countries, professions, creeds) which during the past century has become manifest in the form of two increasingly distinct and irreconcilable human types, those who believe in progress and those who do not – what does this portend except the separation and birth of a new stratum in the biosphere?

b. *Sustenance and reassurance for our power of will.* Through the centuries life has become an increasingly heavy burden for Man the Species, just as it does for Man the Individual as the years pass. The modern world, with its prodigious growth of complexity, weighs incomparably more heavily upon the shoulders of our generation than did the ancient world upon the shoulders of our forebears. Have you never felt that this added load needs to be compensated for by an added passion, a new sense of purpose? To my mind, this is what is 'providentially' arising to sustain our courage – the hope, the belief that some immense fulfilment lies ahead of us.

If mankind were destined to achieve its apotheosis, if Evolution were to reach its highest point in our small separate lives, then indeed the enormous travail of terrestrial organization into which we are born would be no more than a tragic irrelevance. We should all be dupes. We should do better in that case to stop, to call a halt, destroy the machines, close the laboratories, and seek whatever way of escape we can find in pure pleasure or pure nirvana.

But if on the contrary man sees a new door opening above him, a new stage for his development; if each of us can believe that he is working so that the Universe may be raised, in him and through him, to a higher level – then a new spring of energy will well forth in the heart of Earth's workers. The whole great human organism, overcoming a momentary hesitation, will draw its breath and press on with strength renewed.

Indeed, the idea, the hope of the planetization of life is very much more than a mere matter of biological speculation. It is more of a necessity for our age than the discovery, which we so ardently pursue, of new sources of energy. It is this idea which can and must bring us the spiritual fire without which all material fires, so laboriously lighted, will presently die down on the surface of the thinking earth: the fire inspiring us with the joy of action and the zest for life. (F.M., pp. 116–18; Fontana, pp. 120–22.)

III. THE CONVERGENCE OF THE UNIVERSE

It now seems difficult to deny that mankind, after having gradually covered the Earth with a living web of a loose social organization, is now in process of concentrating upon itself (racially, economically, and intellectually) at a continually more rapid pace. The first thing we have to do when we try to explain this process, is to realize that the world of man is being irresistibly forced to form one single whole. It is *converging* upon itself. (A.E. (*Oeuvres* VII), p. 335.)

Far from appearing to be slowing up or reaching its ceiling around us, this biological movement of pan-human convergence has simply been entering (for the last century) into a *compressive phase*, in which it is bound to accelerate from now on. It is conceivable that certain abnormal individuals will exercise their liberty of refusal and break free (to their loss) from this aspiration of the 'evolutionary vortex'. But such evasions can only be viewed as a loss. In fact, on the scale of the species, the process of totalization *cannot*, by its nature, be brought to a halt, linked as it appears to be to two cosmic curves on which our will has no effect: on the one hand, the geometrical curvature of a planet which, relative to our number and radius of action, continues rapidly to contract; and on the other, the psychic curvature of a collective thinking that no force in the world could prevent from concentrating on itself. (A.M., pp. 245–6.)

Nobody, I repeat, can contest this convergence, because everybody is subject to it. On the other hand we have the odd fact that nobody seems to notice it (except to regret it), and nobody seems to suspect that, underlying the complex of historical accidents into which this event may be reduced by analysis, a certain 'force' is undoubtedly at work, as primordial, and as generalized as nuclear forces or gravity, but one that reveals perhaps even more clearly the physical nature of the Universe. (A.E. (*Oeuvres* VII), pp. 335–6.)

We commonly think and speak now of 'an explosive Universe', and when we do so we know very well that we are not leaving the domain of fact and experience.

Surely, however, we may well, and with even more justification, speak of 'a Universe that, as a result of an organic arrangement that is continually carried further, is psychically concentrating and reflecting upon itself'? (Ibid., p. 295.)

There is something more to be seen now in the Universe than the heartbreaking work of entropy, which inexorably reduces all things to the most elementary and stable forms.

Emerging through and above this rain of ashes, there is a sort of cosmic vortex within which the stuff of the world, by a selective use of chance, twists and folds upon itself ever more closely, in more complex and more highly centred forms of association.

We see a world that is balanced upon instability, because it is in constant motion: and a world whose dynamic consistence increases in direct ratio with the complexity of its arrangements, because it is converging upon itself, at as many sidereal points as there have been, as there are, and as there ever will be, thinking planets. (Ibid. p. 303.)

'Structurally and notwithstanding any impression or appearance to the contrary, man is at present engaged in a process within which (by the very use of his liberty, that is to say in order to survive and attain 'super-life') he is compelled (*at least statistically*) to an ever-increasing biological self-unification. Therefore, right in front of us in time, a *peak* of hominization must necessarily exist – a peak which, to judge by the enormous *quantity of unarranged humanity* still all around us, must certainly lie *very far above us* in consciousness, if not so far from us in time as we might at first be tempted to suppose.' (A.M., p. 246.)

IV. THE FINAL EMERGENCE: OMEGA POINT

When we try to examine scientifically what sort of end awaits mankind on earth, I would rather there were less talk of catastrophe (that is a gratuitous and lazy hypothesis), or decay (for we have no reason to believe that the Noosphere may not be immune from the ravages of old age – the evidence is very much the other way) or of astronautic emigration (an escape that is astronomically improbable). On the contrary, we should, I think, look at the problem both more closely and more deeply and then make up our minds to draw the final consequences from this essential fact: that Noogenesis (which is what Anthropogenesis essentially amounts to) is *a convergent phenomenon.* In other words it is, by its nature, directed towards an ending and a completion that is *internal in origin.* And here I can only repeat, pushing its conclusions as far as they can be taken, what has been the constant theme running through what I have already said. If it is true, as I hope I have shown, that the human social phenomenon is simply the higher form assumed on Earth by the involution of the cosmic stuff upon itself, then we must accept something for which the road has been prepared by the emergence (already adumbrated in the sciences) of a *Weltanschauung* common to the consciousness of all mankind. By that I mean that we must recognize the rapidly increasing probability that we are approaching a critical point of maturity, at which man, now completely reflecting upon himself not only individually but collectively, will have reached, along the complexity–axis (and this with the full force of his spiritual impact) the extreme limit of the world. And it is then, if we wish to attribute a significant direction to our experience and see where it leads, that it seems we are obliged to envisage in that direction, finally to round off the phenomenon, the ultimate emergence of thought on earth into what I have called Omega Point. (*Comment je vois,* para. 19.)

5. The Activation of Human Energy

I. HUMAN ENERGY

As Evolution becomes both self-conscious and (at least along its central axis) self-operative in man, so it automatically *can foresee its future*.

That is all that is required to bring to light the formidable problem of the *impetus of Evolution*, in addition to and at a higher level than questions of structure and process that sufficed until now to cover the economy of nature. It is a biological problem of a new type; it silently raises itself in our hearts, and is well on the way to dominating in the near future the other more general problem (itself becoming more urgent on all sides), that of at last constructing an *energetics of man*. (A.E. (*Oeuvres* VII), p. 348.)

By the energy of man I here mean the always increasing portion of cosmic energy at present undergoing the recognizable influence of the centres of human activity.

In the elementary state (that is to say considered within and around an isolated human element) this 'hominized' energy appears in three forms, at first sight diverse, which it is interesting to distinguish, at least for convenience' sake: incorporated energy, controlled energy, spiritualized energy.

a. *Incorporated energy* is that which the slow biological evolution of the earth has gradually accumulated and harmonized in our organism of flesh and nerves: the astonishing 'natural machine' of the human body.

b. *Controlled energy* is energy around him which man ingeniously succeeds in dominating with physical power originating from his limbs by means of 'artificial machines'.

c. *Spiritualized energy*, lastly, is localized in the immanent zones of our free activity, and forms the stuff of our intellectual processes, affections and volitions. This energy is probably incapable of measurement, but is very real all the same, since it gains a reflective and passionate mastery of things and their relationships.

These three types of energy, as I said, seem at first sight to form heterogeneous categories. In reality, it appears difficult on reflection to find a sharp boundary between them. . . .

By all appearances, in fact, every human individual seems to represent a cosmic nucleus of a special nature, radiating around it waves of organization and excitation within matter. Just such a nucleus, with its halo of animation around it, is the unit of human energy.

Let us now consider human energy as a whole.

This energy is created at every moment by the sum of all the elementary energies accumulated on the earth's surface.[1] (H.E., pp. 115–16.)

Being in the forefront of the cosmic wave of advance, the energy of man assumes an importance disproportionate to its apparently small size. Compared with the magnitude of the stars, the Noosphere is an almost insignificant film. In reality this thin surface is nothing less than the most progressive form under which it has been given to us to apprehend and contemplate the energy of the Universe. This tenuous envelope holds the secret essence of the vastnesses that it fringes: the highest note reached by the vibration of worlds.

The meaning of this is twofold:

First, that the *direction* of advance so far followed by the

[1] The energy of the Noosphere.

cosmos is indicated to us by the human spearhead. Consequently, by analysing the conditions of our activity, we can hope to discover the fundamental conditions which govern the general functioning of the universe.

Second, that in *magnitude* we hold, concentrated in the human mass, the most living, quintessential treasure and hope of the world. (H.E., p. 121.)

II. THE COSMIC PROBLEM OF ACTION AND THE PERSONAL OPTION

One of the most important aspects of hominization, from the point of view of the history of life, is the accession of biological realities (or values) to the domain of moral realities (or values). From man onwards and in man, evolution has taken reflective consciousness of itself. Henceforth it can to some degree recognize its position in the world, choose its direction, and withhold its efforts. These new conditions open on earth the immense question of duty and its modalities. Why act – and how to act? . . .

In the development of life up to man, the individual seems always to have been definitely subordinated to the species. Its principal value was that of an agent of transmission, a point on the road. Life's task, it seems, was to achieve, by means of increasingly organized elements, the establishment on earth of a higher form of consciousness, a *state of personality*. With man and in man, the perfected and centred element, that is to say the *person*, is finally constituted. Will not values find their centre of gravity shifted by this basic event? Up to that point the unit existed for the mass. Henceforth will not the mass exist for the unit? . . . Let the human individual, newly arrived on the great waters of life, enjoy in his first moment of exaltation the intoxication of *raising himself to* the highest point of the Universe. The temptation is quite natural. But let him beware! Despite, or rather because of the autonomy he has attained, he is always dominated by another, higher unity from which he cannot free himself on pain of death. Precious though it is, the human monad remains vitally subjected to the law that, before his coming, obliged units to preserve and promote the whole in preference to themselves. (H.E., pp. 29–31.)

The energy of man, as we have just recognized, comes to our notice as the last factor of a vast process in which the total mass of the Universe is engaged. . . . Around us and in us the energy of man, itself sustained by the energy of the Universe of which it is the crown, is still pursuing its mysterious progress towards higher states of thought and freedom. Willy-nilly, we are totally caught up in this transformation. I repeat my question, therefore: 'What shall we do? Resist the current?' This would be foolish and, moreover, impossible. Let ourselves be passively carried along by the wave? This would be cowardice. And anyhow, how can we remain neutral, since our essence is to act? Only one way remains open to us: to trust in the infallibility and finally beatifying value of the action in which we are involved. In us the world's evolution towards spirit has become conscious. Our perfection, our interest, our salvation as elements can depend therefore on nothing less than pushing this evolution forward with all our strength. We may not yet understand exactly where it is taking us, but it is absurd for us to doubt that it is leading us towards some end of supreme value.

Hence it is that, *for the first time* since the awakening of life on earth, the fundamental problem of action has finally emerged into our human consciousness in the twentieth century. Up to now man has acted principally out of instinct, from day to day, without much knowledge of why or for whom he was working. Contemporaneously with the flowing into him of fresh powers, a new limitless and immeasurable field of activity is opened for his ambitions and, in some sense, for his worship. For anyone who has understood (and everyone will inevitably do so soon) the position and significance of the smallest portion of thought in nature, the fundamental matter has become one of rationally assuring the progress of the world of which we form part. No longer only, as of old, for our little individuality, our little family, our little country – no longer indeed only for the whole earth – but for the salvation and success of the Universe itself, how should we modern men best organize the maintenance, distribution and progress of the energy of man around us?

Therein lies the whole question. (H.E., pp. 121–5.)

III. THE ACTIVATION OF HUMAN ENERGY:
OMEGA POINT

It is not enough, in fact, that man has at his disposal the requisite power to become synthesized beyond himself. He must also *have the will* to do so. And for that he must have the *taste* for going further; that is to say, under the influence of a sort of internal 'gravitation', he must be *drawn* upwards, from within. Humanity, devoid of this taste, humanity not drawn towards 'more being', would infallibly and rapidly become extinct; even astronomical piles of calories placed in his hands would not save him.

Now what is necessary, if we are to agree not only joyfully but passionately to push on the increasingly heavy and complicated work that cosmic synthesis requires of us? What conditions must the Universe absolutely fulfil in order that we may be drawn towards ever greater consciousness?

a. *Irreversibility*

This (according to all those who have tried to discover the psychological mechanism of action) is the condition; that we shall not imagine the movement that beckons us forward to be condemned in advance to stop or draw back. We must know that it is, by nature, *irreversible*. Promise man as many million years as you will. Let him glimpse at the end of the period as high (that is to say as superhuman) a summit as you will. If it is known beforehand that, once that summit is reached, we shall have to descend without any signs of our ascent surviving in the Universe; then, I say plainly, we shall not have the heart to advance, and we shall not advance. . . . Man will never consent to labour like a Sisyphus. (V.P., pp. 230–1.)

With the germ of consciousness hatched upon its surface, the Earth, our perishable earth threatened by the final, absolute zero, has brought into the Universe a demand, henceforth irrepressible, not only that all things shall not die, but that what is best in the world, that which has become most complex, most highly centred, shall be saved. It is through human consciousness, genetically linked to a heavenly body whose days are ultimately numbered, that Evolution proclaims its challenge: either it must be irreversible, or it need not go on at all! Man the individual consoles himself for his passing with the thought of the offspring or the works which he leaves behind. But what will presently be left of mankind?

Thus every attempt to situate Man and the Earth in the framework of the Universe comes inevitably upon the serious problem of death, not of the individual but on the planetary scale – a death which, if we seriously anticipate it, must instantly, here and now, paralyse all the vital forces of the Earth. (F.M., p. 121; Fontana, pp. 125–6.)

In order to balance our conceptions of the Universe it is not enough, therefore, to arrest the 'curve of moleculization' at the formation even of a planetary consciousness. It is, moreover, impossible to suppose that, like the lines of space it will curve backwards by way of refraction. By virtue of the new conditions imposed on it by the appearance and demands of reflective thought, capable of criticizing its future and refusing to progress, men must agree that its trajectory will definitely leap forward in the direction of a supreme place of personalizing centration and consolidation. (V.P., p. 231.)

b. *Unanimity and Personality*

The first essential is that the human units involved in the process shall draw closer together, not merely under the pressure of *external* forces, or solely by the performance of material acts, but directly, centre to centre, through *internal* attraction. Not through coercion, or enslavement to a common task, but through *unanimity* in a common spirit. The construction of molecules ensues through atomic affinity. Similarly, on a higher level, it is through *sympathy*, and this alone, that the human elements in a personalized universe may hope to rise to the level of a higher synthesis.

It is a matter of common experience that within restricted groups (the pair, the team) unity, far from diminishing the individual, enhances, enriches and liberates him in terms of himself. True union, the union of heart and spirit, does not enslave, nor does it neutralize the individuals which it brings together. It *super-personalizes* them. Let us try to picture the phenomenon on a terrestrial scale. Imagine men awakening at last, under the influence of the ever-tightening planetary embrace, to a sense of universal solidarity based on their profound community, evolutionary in its nature and purpose. The nightmares of brutalization and mechanization which are conjured up to terrify us and prevent our advance are at once dispelled. It is not harshness or hatred, but a new kind of love, not yet experienced by man, which we must learn to look for as it is borne to us on the rising tide of planetization.

Reflecting, even briefly, on the state of affairs which might evoke this new universal love in the human heart, a love so often vainly dreamed of, but which now leaves the fields of Utopia to reveal itself as both possible and necessary, we are brought to the following conclusion: that for men upon earth, all the earth, to learn to love one another, it is not enough that they should know themselves to be members of one and the same *thing*; in 'planetizing' themselves they must acquire the consciousness, without losing themselves, of becoming one and the same *person*. For there is no total love that does not proceed from, and exist within, that which is personal. (F.M., pp. 119–20; Fontana, pp. 123–4.)

An (irreversible) centre of personal stuff totalizing in itself the essence of our personalities; this comes to be the definition, as we gradually see it more clearly, of the universal centre of attraction, recognized as necessary if the impetus of the Noosphere is to be sustained. (H.E., p. 142.)

Let us suppose that from this universal centre, the Omega Point, there constantly emanate radiations hitherto only perceptible to those persons whom we call 'mystics'. Let us further imagine that, as the sensibility or response to mysticism of the human race increases with planetization, the awareness of Omega becomes so widespread as to warm the earth psychically while physically it is growing cold. Is it not conceivable that mankind, at the end of its totalization, its folding-in upon itself, may reach a critical point of maturity where, leaving Earth and stars to lapse slowly back into the dwindling mass of primordial energy, it will detach itself from this planet and join the one true, irreversible essence of things, the Omega Point? A phenomenon perhaps outwardly akin to death; but in reality a simple metamorphosis and arrival at the supreme synthesis. An escape from the planet, not in space or outwardly, but spiritually and inwardly, such as the hyper-concentration of cosmic matter upon itself allows.

This hypothesis of a final maturing and ecstasy of mankind, the logical conclusion of the theory of complexity, may seem even more far-fetched than the idea (of which it is the extension) of the planetization of Life. Yet it holds its ground and grows stronger upon reflection. It is in harmony with the growing importance which leading thinkers of all types are beginning to attach to the phenomenon of mysticism. In any event, of all the theories which we may evolve concerning the end of the Earth, it is the only one which affords a coherent prospect wherein, in the remote future, the deepest and most powerful currents of human consciousness may converge and culminate: intelligence and action, science and religion. (F.M., pp. 122–3; Fontana, pp. 127–8.)

IV. LOVE AS ENERGY

In us and around us, we have been able to conclude, the world's units are continually and increasingly personalizing, by approaching a goal of unification, itself personal; in such a way that the world's essential energy radiates from this goal and finally flows back towards it; having confusedly set the cosmic mass in motion, it emerges from it to form the Noosphere.

What name should we give to an influence of this sort?

Only one is possible: love.

Love is by definition the word we use for attractions of a personal nature. Since once the Universe has become a thinking one everything in the last resort moves in and towards personality, it is necessarily love, a kind of love, which forms and will increasingly form, in its pure state, the material of human energy. (H.E., pp. 145-6.)

Love is the most universal, the most tremendous and the most mysterious of the cosmic forces. . . .

From the standpoint of spiritual evolution, which we here assume, it seems that we can give a name and value to this strange energy of love. Can we not say quite simply that in its essence it is the attraction exercised on each unit of consciousness by the centre of the Universe in course of taking shape? It calls us to the great union, the realization of which is the only process at present taking place in nature. By this hypothesis, according to which (in agreement with the findings of psychological analysis) love is the primal and universal psychic energy, does not everything become clear around us, both for our minds and our actions? . . .

'Hominized' love is distinct from all other love, because the 'spectrum' of its warm and penetrating light is marvellously enriched. No longer only a unique and periodic attraction for purposes of material fertility; but an unbounded and continuous possibility of contact between minds rather than bodies; the play of countless subtle antennae seeking one another in the light and darkness of the soul; the pull towards mutual sensibility and completion, in which preoccupation with preserving the species gradually dissolves in the greater intoxication of two people creating a world. It is a fact, that through woman the universe advances towards man. The whole question (the vital question for the earth) is that they shall recognize one another.

If man fails to recognize the true nature, the true object, of his love the confusion is vast and irremediable. Bent on assuaging a passion intended for the All on an object too small to satisfy it, he will strive to compensate a fundamental imbalance by materialism or an ever-increasing multiplicity of experiments. His efforts will be fruitless – and in the eyes of one who can see the inestimable value of the 'spiritual quantum' of man, a terrible waste. But let us put aside any sentimental feelings or virtuous indignation. Let us look very coolly as biologists or engineers, at the lurid atmosphere of our great towns at evening. There, and everywhere else as well, the earth is continually dissipating its most marvellous power. This is pure loss. Earth is burning away, wasted on the empty air. How much energy do you think the spirit of the earth loses in a single night?

If only man would turn and see the reality of the Universe shining in the spirit and through the flesh. He would then discover the reason for what has hitherto deceived and perverted his powers of love. Woman stands before him as the lure and symbol of the world. He cannot embrace her except by himself growing, in his turn, to a world scale. And because the world is always growing and always unfinished and always ahead of us, to achieve his love man is engaged in a limitless conquest of the universe and himself. In this sense, man can only attain woman by consummating a union with the Universe. Love is a sacred reserve of energy; it is like the blood of spiritual evolution. (H.E., pp. 32–4.)

We have already several times stressed the capital truth that 'union differentiates'. Love is only the concrete expression of this metaphysical principle. Let us imagine an earth on which human beings were primarily (and even in a sense exclusively) concerned with achieving global accession to a passionately desired universal being, whom each one would recognize as a living presence in the most incommunicable features of his neighbour. In such a world, constraint would become useless as a means of keeping individuals in the most favourable condition for action, of guiding them in free competition towards better social groupings, of making them accept the restrictions and sacrifices imposed by a certain human selection, of deciding them once and for all not to waste their power of love but to raise it carefully and husband it for the final union. Under these conditions life would finally escape (supreme liberation) from the tyranny of material coercions; and a personality of increasing freedom would grow up without opposition within the totality. (H.E., pp. 152–3.)

Totalization of total human energy in a total love.

The ideal glimpsed in their dreams by the world technicians.

This, psychologically, is what love can do if carried to a universal degree.

But is this miracle *really* moving towards realization? (H.E., p. 155.)

Père Teilhard answers this question in the affirmative, saying that 'some traces of this prodigious transformation must be perceptible in history'.

This will constitute one of his approaches to the Christian problem. In his view, there can be no possible doubt: 'Christianity is precisely a phylum of love in Nature.' *The complete series of apologetical arguments for Christianity will be given again in Part 2 (comparison of religions).*

Finally, Père Teilhard adds this suggestion:

At two critical points human energy has already assumed the form in which we know it today: first the appearance of life, whence emerged the biosphere; then emergence of thought which produced the Noosphere.

Cannot a further and final metamorphosis have been in progress since the birth of love in Christianity: the coming to consciousness of an 'Omega' in the heart of the Noosphere – the circles' motion towards their common centre: *the appearance of the 'Theosphere'*?

A dream and a fantasy, it will be said. But it fits singularly well with the march of things (H.E., p. 160.)

V. SUMMARY

At the same time this convergent phenomenon is also in virtue of its structure, irreversible in nature: in this sense, that once Evolution has become reflective and free, in Man, it can no longer continue its ascent towards complexity-consciousness unless it realizes two things about 'vital involution' – that, looking ahead, it escapes annihilation or total death, and, what is more, that it gathers together all that can be permanently saved of the essence of what life will have given birth to in the course of its progress. This demand for irreversibility has a structural implication, the existence, at the upper term of cosmic convergence, of a transcendent centre of unification, 'Omega Point'. Unless this focus-point, which gathers things together and ensures their irreversibility, does in fact exist, the law of evolutionary recurrence cannot hold good to the very end.

6. A Summary of my Phenomenological View of the World

As a conclusion to this first part (which Teilhard called his 'phenomenology') we give the statement which he sent to Claude Tresmontant and Jeanne Mortier (see Introduction, p. 12).

The starting point and key of the whole system

'Developing as a counter-current that cuts across Entropy, there is a cosmic drift of matter towards states of arrangement of progressively greater complexity (this being towards – or within – a "third infinite", *the infinite of complexity*, which is just as real as the Infinitesimal or the Immense). And consciousness presents itself to our experience as the effect or the *specific* property of this Complexity taken to extremely high values.'

If this law of recurrence (I call it the law of 'complexity-consciousness') is applied to the history of the World, we see the emergence of an ascending series of critical points and outstanding developments, which are the following.

1. Critical point of vitalization

Somewhere, at the level of the proteins, an initial emergence of consciousness is produced within the pre-living (at least so far as our experience goes). And, by virtue of the accompanying mechanism of 'reproduction', the rise of complexity on earth increases its pace *phyletically* (the genesis of species or speciation).

Starting from this stage (and in the case of the higher living beings) it becomes possible to 'measure' the advance of organic complexification by the progress of cerebration. That device enables us to distinguish, within the biosphere, a specially favoured axis of complexity–consciousness: that of the Primates.

2. *Critical point of reflection (or hominization)*

As a result of some 'hominizing' cerebral mutation, which appears among the Anthropoids towards the end of the Tertiary period, psychic reflection – not simply *knowing*, but *knowing that one knows* – bursts upon the world and opens up an entirely new domain for Evolution. With man (apparently no more than a new zoological 'family') it is in fact a *second species of life* that begins (the Noosphere).

3. *Development of Co-reflection (and rise of an ultra-human)*

If it is applied to the great phenomenon of human socialization, the criterion of complexity–consciousness provides some decisive evidence. On the one hand, an irresistible and irreversible technico-cultural organization, noospheric in dimension, is manifestly in progress of development within human society. On the other hand, as an effect of Co-reflection, the human mind is continually rising up collectively – collectively, because of the links forged by technology – to the appreciation of new dimensions: for example, the evolutionary organicity and corpuscular structure of the Universe. Here the *coupling* of organization and interiorization can again be very clearly distinguished. This means that all around us the fundamental process of Cosmogenesis is continuing just as before (or even with renewed vigour).

Considered as a zoological whole, mankind is presenting the unique spectacle of a phylum that is organico–psychically synthesizing upon itself. It is, indeed, a 'corpusculization' and a 'centration' (or centring) upon itself of the Noosphere *as a whole*.[1]

4. *Probability of a critical point of Ultra-reflection ahead of us*

If it is extrapolated into the future, mankind's technico-socio-mental convergence upon itself forces us to envisage a climax of Co-reflection, at some finite distance in time ahead of us: for this we can find no better (indeed, no other) definition than a critical point of Ultra-reflection. We cannot, of course, either imagine or describe such a phenomenon, which would seem to imply an escape from Space and Time. Nevertheless there are certain precise conditions in the field of energy that must be satisfied by the event we anticipate (a more pronounced awakening in man, as it comes closer, of the 'zest for evolution' and the 'will to live'); and from these we are forced to conclude that Ultra-reflection coincides with a final attainment of irreversibility. This must be so, since the prospect of a total death would be so disheartening as to stop the further development of hominization.

It is to this higher term of Co-reflection (which means in fact, of unanimization) that I have given the name of 'Omega Point': the cosmic, personalizing, centre of unification and union.

5. *The likelihood of a reaction (or 'reflection') of Omega on the Human in the course of Co-reflection (Revelation and the Christian phenomenon)*

The more we consider the indispensability of an Omega to maintain and animate the continued progress of hominized Evolution, the more clearly can we see two things.

[1] Teilhard uses the English phrase, *as a whole*.

The first is that a purely conjectural Omega – one that was arrived at simply by 'calculation' – would be powerless to keep active in man's heart a passion strong enough to make him continue the process of hominization to the very end.

The second is that if Omega does really exist, it is difficult not to accept that its supreme 'Ego' in some way makes itself felt as such by all the imperfect Egos (that is to say all the reflective elements) of the Universe.

From this point of view the ancient and traditional idea of 'Revelation' reappears and again finds a place in Cosmogenesis – entering it, this time, through biology and the energetics of evolution.

From this point of view, again, the Christian mystical current takes on an extraordinary significance and actuality: and this because, while it is true that, by the logic of energetics, the heart of some intense faith is absolutely indispensable to the completion of the process of complexity-consciousness, at the same time it is equally true (how true, you have only to look around the world to realize) that at the present moment no faith can be distinguished that is capable of fully taking over (by 'amorizing' it) a convergent Cosmogenesis, except faith in a Christ, a Christ of the Pleroma and Parousia, *in quo omnia constant*, in whom all things find their consistence.

New York, 14 January 1954.

Note: this fifth section is more properly a summary of the apologetical dialectic presented in Part 2, where it will accordingly reappear (see p. 108). It has been printed above in order to give the reader Père Teilhard's statement as an integral whole.

Part Two

Apologetics

Père Teilhard de Chardin regarded apologetics as a dialectical process aimed at identifying the cosmic Christ of Christian revelation with Omega Point arrived at by phenomenological extrapolation (and thereby providing a proof and defence of the truth of Christianity). Such is the definition he gives in the summary of his thought (p. 145):

It is upon this 'Physics' that, in a 'second phase', Père Teilhard builds first an apologetics: under the illuminating influence of Grace, our minds recognize in the unifying properties of the Christian phenomenon a manifestation of Omega, a reflection of Omega upon human consciousness, and so identify the Omega of reason with the Universal Christ of revelation.

One can hardly bring a charge of Concordism against such an approach. A little later, Père Teilhard makes this perfectly clear:

... Concordism and coherence should not be confused. Religion and science obviously represent two different meridians on the mental sphere, and it would be wrong not to keep them separate (that is the concordist mistake); but these meridians must necessarily meet somewhere at a pole of common vision (that is, coherence). Otherwise all that is ours in the domain of consciousness collapses.

Finally, in his Outline of a Dialectic of Spirit (1946, in A. E. (Oeuvres VII)), Père Teilhard defines with remarkable clarity the different steps in this apologetics. It emerges as a dialectic, in other words a dialogue in which the intelligence reflects alternately on what it already knows (phenomenology) and what it seeks to know (hypotheses, in the domain of energetics and philosophy, relating to Omega). It is from this essay that we have taken the structural arrangement of this second part.

In order to avoid any misunderstanding, I think I shall do well to set out my apologetics, clearly broken down into its successive phases. (A.E. (*Oeuvres* VII), p. 149.)

1. The Attributes of Omega Point: a Transcendent God

I. IRREVERSIBILITY

One point at least seems capable of being established by *analysis of the present facts*; and this is that unless we make up our minds to admit that the cosmos is intrinsically an absurdity, the growth of the spirit must be taken as irreversible. 'The spirit *as a whole* will never fall back.' In other words, 'In an evolutionary universe, the existence of spirit by its nature rules out the possibility of a death in which the achievements of the spirit will *totally* disappear or, to be more precise, in which they will not survive in *the form of their flowering*.' Such is the infinitely comforting guarantee afforded us by these few words which express a stroke of immediate and fundamental intuition:

'The world would justifiably and infallibly cease to act – out of discouragement – if it became aware (in its thinking zones) that it is going to be a total death. Therefore *total death does not exist*.'

This argument will, I know, appear suspect to many. Many thinkers, after the example of H. Poincaré, accepting a fashionable agnosticism or seduced by the false lure of stoicism or a very fine altruism, believe that they can accept without weakening the idea that thought on earth will last only a moment, and that we must devote everything to that moment, which is 'a lightning-flash in the night'. These thinkers have, I believe, deluded themselves by not following to its conclusion the significance of this phrase: *total death* of the universe. Unconsciously, I am certain, they stop short of finding the full meaning of the words they use. They are assuming that some trace of this 'lightning-flash' will remain; something will be preserved by a consciousness, a memory, a glance. But even this last hope must be abandoned if the idea of absolute death (probably as absurd as the idea of nothingness) is to be given its full force. No, not even a trace. (It would still mean everything to the Universe even for an instant to have cast its spell on an observer who will retain that vision for ever!) Around us total, impenetrable darkness, which will let *nothing* of all we have understood and achieved filter through to *anyone*. Then why make efforts? Why follow the orders and expectations of evolution? Out of supreme altruism? But there is no virtue in sacrifice when no higher interest is at stake. A universe which would continue *to act laboriously* in the conscious expectation of absolute death would be a stupid world, a spiritual monstrosity, in fact a chimera. Now since in fact the world appears before us here and now as one huge action perpetually taking place with formidable assurance, there can be no doubt at all that it is capable of nourishing indefinitely in its offspring an appetite for life, which is continually growing more critical, exacting and refined. It must carry within it the guarantees of ultimate success. *From the moment that it admits thought, a universe can no longer be simply temporary or of limited evolution: it must by its very structure emerge into the absolute.*[1] (H.E., pp. 40–1.)

To ward off the threat of disappearance, incompatible with the mechanism of reflective activity, man tries to bring together in an ever vaster and more permanent sub-

[1] Editor's italics.

ject the collective principle of his acquisitions – civilization, humanity, the spirit of the earth. Associated in these enormous entities, with their incredibly slow rhythm of evolution, he has the impression of having escaped the destructive action of time.

But by doing so he has only pushed back the problem. For after all, however large the radius traced within time and space, does the circle ever embrace anything but the perishable? So long as our constructions rest with all their weight on the earth, they will vanish with the earth. The radical defect in all forms of belief in progress, as they are expressed in positivist credos, is that they do not definitively eliminate death. What is the use of detecting a focus of any sort in the van of evolution, if that focus can and must one day disintegrate? To satisfy the ultimate requirements of our action, Omega must be independent of the collapse of the forces with which evolution is woven. (P.M., pp. 269–70; Fontana, pp. 296–7.)

II. PERSONALITY

If human particles are to group themselves 'centrically' they must ultimately – in unison and simultaneously – love one another; for there is no true love in an atmosphere of collectivity, that is to say, that is impersonal.

Love cannot be born, and take permanent root, unless it finds a heart, a face. (*Comment je vois*, para. 20 c.)

The personality of God (together with the survival of the 'soul') calls out the greatest opposition and antipathy from contemporary scientific thought. The origin of this dislike is to be found in the intellectual contempt which has rejected as 'anthropocentric' all attempts to understand the Universe through man. Let us once more put the fact of man in its true place. Let us recognize, not out of vanity or idleness but on scientific evidence, that no phenomenon has had more preparation, or is more axial and characteristic than this. And at the same time we are compelled to admit that even (and particularly) today, because of the new value Man is assuming in Nature, the idea of a God conceived as a distinct and animate centre of the world, is necessarily in full growth. Let us say, in fact, substituting one equivalent formula for another, that by the capital event of *hominization*, the most advanced portion of the cosmos has become *personalized*. This simple change of variable brings in sight, for the future, a double condition of existence which is quite inevitable.

First of all, since everything *in the Universe beyond man* takes place within *personalized being*, the final divine term of universal convergence must also (eminently) possess the quality of a Person (without which it would be inferior to the elements it governs). But there is a further observation to be made, a little subtler but no less certain. To the idea of a personal (or rather super-personal) centre emerging from Multiplicity, we at first react by imagining this centre as forming itself from the legacy or 'remains' of inferior centres of personality which surrender their progress to it. Now this is an inaccurate view, and arises from the fact that we transfer unaltered into *the personalized sphere of the World* a type of heredity peculiar to infra-personal zones of the cosmos. Let us reflect further, and we shall recognize that a *person* can only transmit (and can only have the vital desire to transmit) *its own personality* to evolution. We imagine that by the progress of cosmic Being, this person becomes 'super-centred', or centred not on itself but on a higher being. But it would not be possible for it to pass to this centre as a gift presented by itself, *which would not be itself.* For its whole quality lies in *being itself* – the incommunicable expression of a conscious observation point upon the universe. If this is the case, the final summit of the perfected – that is to say per-sonalized – World (that is to say God) can in no way be con-ceived as born of a sort of aggregation of elementary per-sonalities (since these are, by nature, irremovable from their own centres). In order to *super-animate without destroying* a Universe formed of personal elements, it must be a special Centre itself.[1] (H.E., pp. 45–6.)

III. REALITY AND ACTUALITY

Love, I said, dies in contact with the impersonal and the anonymous. With equal infallibility, it becomes impoverished with remoteness in space – and still more, much more, with difference in time. For love to be possible, there must be co-existence. Accordingly, however marvellous its foreseen figure, Omega could never even so much as equilibrate the play of human attractions and repulsions if it did not act with equal force, that is to say with the same stuff of prox-imity. With love, as with every other sort of energy, it is within the existing datum that the lines of force must at every instant come together. Neither an ideal centre, nor a potential centre could possibly suffice. An actual and real noosphere goes with a real and actual Centre. To be supremely attractive Omega must already be supremely present. (P.M., p. 269; Fontana, p. 296.)

[1] i.e. a Person.

IV. AUTONOMY, TRANSCENDENCE

While being the last term of the evolutionary series, Omega is also *outside* all series. Not only does it crown, but it closes. Otherwise the sum total of the process would collapse upon itself – in organic contradiction with the whole operation. When, going beyond the elements, we come to speak of the conscious Pole of the world, it is not enough to say that it *emerges* from the rise of consciousness: we must add that from this genesis it has already *emerged*; without which it could neither subjugate into love nor fix in incorruptibility. If by its very nature it did not escape from the time and space which gathers it together, it would not be Omega. (P.M., pp. 270–1; Fontana, p. 297.)

It is impossible to justify evolution through increasing complexity – the laborious climb towards the improbable – without imagining that somewhere, making itself felt in the very heart of evolution, there is 'a centre that is sufficiently independent and active to force, when it so requires, the whole of the cosmic layer to centre (i.e. to complexify) itself in the likeness of that centre'. (*Comment je vois*, para. 20 b.)

Unless Omega were in some way emancipated from time and space, it could not already be present for us nor could it be the basis for our hopes of irreversibility. Thus, in one of its aspects, different from that in which we are witnessing its formation, it has always been emerging above a world from which, seen from another angle, it is, at the same time, in process of emergence. (A.E. (*Oeuvres* VII), p. 119.)

Multiplicity ascends, attracted and engulfed by something which is 'already One'. This is the secret and guarantee of the irreversibility of life. (H.E., p. 46.)

2. Evolutionary Creation and the Expectation of a Revelation

I. EVOLUTIONARY CREATION

It is from this centre of irreversibility, once discovered, that the light breaks backwards, illuminating the hidden mechanism of the phenomenon. At first, we could only note with astonishment, but not explain, the persistent rise of a fraction of the world, against the current, towards ever more improbable states of complexity. Now we see that this paradoxical movement is sustained by a prime mover ahead. The branch climbs, not supported by its base but suspended from the future. This is what renders the movement not only irreversible but irresistible. From this point of view (which is that not only of simple antecedence, but of causality itself) evolution assumes its true figure for our mind and our heart. It is certainly not 'creative', as science for a brief moment believed; but it is the expression of creation, for our experience, in time and space. (V.P., p. 231.)

If, as we ascend, Omega is seen from our side of things, at first it stands out on the horizon as a centre of convergence that is no more than immanent: mankind totally reflected upon itself. But when we come to examine it, it becomes plain that if this focus point is to hold firm it presupposes behind it, and at a deeper level, a transcendent – divine – nucleus.

If the Multiple becomes unified, it is ultimately because it is subject to a force of attraction. (A.E. (*Oeuvres* VII), pp. 152–3.)

85

II. THE EXPECTATION OF A REVELATION

In an initial phase – before man – the attraction was vitally but blindly received by the world. Since man's coming, it has become at least partially conscious in the form of reflective freedom, and it has given rise to religion.

If, as we have admitted, Omega is already *in existence* and *operative* at the very core of the thinking mass, then it would seem inevitable that its existence should be manifested to us here and now through some definite indication. To animate evolution in its lower stages, the conscious pole of the world could of course act only in an impersonal form under the veil of biology. Upon the thinking entity that we have become by hominization, it is now possible for it to radiate from the one Centre to all centres – *personally*. Would it seem likely that it should not do so? (P.M., pp. 291–2; Fontana, pp. 319–20.)

And in consequence we are now led again to find God at the head, in a deeper sense:

Not only . . . as the prime physical or biological mover but as the prime psychical mover, appealing, in us men, to what is most human in us, our intelligence, our heart, and our power of choice.

Ultimately, this means that we have to answer the question whether there may not be, as yet overlooked by us, a hidden *message* in the complex flood of evolutionary forces that run through us. (A.E. (*Oeuvres* VII), p. 153.)

Either the whole construction of the world presented here is vain speculation, or somewhere around us, in one form or another, some excess of personal, extra-human energy must be perceptible to us if we look carefully, and must reveal to us the great Presence. (P.M., p. 292; Fontana, p. 320.)

3. The Christian Phenomenon and Faith
in the Incarnation

I. THE RELIGIOUS PHENOMENON

The idea came to be widely accepted during the nineteenth century that religions express a primitive state of mankind that has now been left behind. 'In former times men developed the concept of divinity in their imaginations in order to account for natural phenomena of whose causes they were ignorant. By discovering the empirical explanation of these same phenomena, science has made God and religions superfluous.' That sums up the new creed of many of our contemporaries. (S.C., p. 98.)

Our generation and the two that preceded it have heard little but talk of the conflict between science and faith; indeed it seemed at one moment a foregone conclusion that the former was destined to take the place of the latter.

But, as the tension is prolonged, the conflict visibly seems to need to be resolved in terms of an entirely different form of equilibrium – not in elimination, or duality, but in synthesis. After close on two centuries of passionate struggle, neither science nor faith has succeeded in discrediting its adversary. On the contrary it is becoming obvious that neither can develop normally without the other. And the reason is simple: the same life animates both ... Religion and science are the two conjugated faces or phases of one and the same complete act of knowledge – the only one which can embrace the past and future of evolution and so contemplate, measure and fulfil them. (P.M., pp. 283–4, 285; Fontana, 311, 312–13.)

Religion is not a strictly individual crisis – or choice or intuition – but represents the long disclosure of God's being through the collective experience of the whole of humanity, God reflecting himself personally on the organized sum of thinking monads, to guarantee an assured success and fix precise laws for their hesitant activities – God bent over the now intelligent mirror of Earth to impress on it the first marks of his Beauty. (H.E., p. 47.)

II. COMPARISON OF RELIGIONS

The development of Mankind requires a religion that will give form to the free psychic energy of the world: one, that is to say, that makes itself felt as a process of construction and conquest that leads up to some supreme unification of the Universe. (S.C., p. 104).

The true God must therefore possess all the attributes ascribed to Omega Point, and must in particular satisfy these two conditions: he must be:

a. A God of cosmic synthesis in whom we can be conscious of advancing and of joining together by spiritual transformation of all powers of matter.

b. A supremely personal God, from whom we are the more distinguishable the more we lose ourselves in Him. (H.E., p. 109.)

If we apply this double criterion to the numerous types of religious, and even secular moral systems, that have followed one another *uninterruptedly* throughout history, they all go up in smoke. Just as practically nothing survives factually beyond its own time, so practically nothing can stand up logically.

The first to be eliminated, at one sweep, are the various

forms of agnosticism, explicit or implicit, that have tried to base morality on a pure social empiricism or again on a pure individual aestheticism, emphatically ruling out any faith in some future consummation of the world. Apart from the individual shortcomings of these various systems, they all have the common fault of cutting off the flow of the life-sap which they should direct into the proper channel and help to rise. Neither Confucianism, which ensured the smooth running of society without progress – nor the wisdom of Marcus Aurelius, whose thought was a bright flower in the garden of mankind – nor the cult, so popular again today, of *self-contained* personal enjoyment and interior perfection – none of these can any longer come up in any way to our ideal of men as builders and conquerors. It is upon a heaven that we must be urged to launch our attack: *if not, we lay down our arms.*

If we turn to the group represented by Islam, nothing has permanence; everything evaporates, and perhaps even more completely. Islam has retained the idea of the existence and the greatness of God. That, it is true, is the seed from which everything may one day be born again; but at the same time Islam has achieved the extraordinary feat of making this God as ineffective and sterile as a non-being for all that concerns the knowledge and betterment of the world. After destroying a great deal and creating locally an ephemeral beauty, Islam offers itself today as a principle of fixation and stagnation. An improvement upon this practical impotence would be perfectly conceivable, and – *basically amounting to a convergence towards Christianity* – already appears to be coming about in a group of high-minded thinkers alive to modern requirements.[1]

[1] Written in 1933.

Next we turn to the imposing mass of Hindu and eastern mystical systems. The East, the first shrine, and, we are assured, the ever-living dwelling-place of the Spirit. The East, where so many from the West still dream of finding shelter for their faith in life. . . . Let us take a closer look at those mighty constructions; and, without even venturing into the temple to savour what sort of incense still burns within it, let us, not as archaeologists or poets, but as architects of the future, examine the solidity of its walls. The very moment we come into fundamental contact with Asia there can be no question of doubt. Those impressive columns are utterly incapable of supporting the drive of our world in these days. The incomparable greatness of the religions of the East lies in their having been second to none in vibrating with the passion for unity. This note, which is essential to every form of mysticism, has even penetrated them so deeply that we find ourselves falling under a spell simply by uttering the names of their Gods. However, the Hindu sages thought that if man is to attain this unity he must renounce the earth, its passions and cares, and the effort it demands. (S.C., pp. 104–5.)

For the Hindu sage, spirit is the homogeneous unity in which the complete adept is lost to self, all individual features and values being suppressed. All quest for knowledge, all personalization, all earthly progress are so many diseases of the soul, *Matter is dead weight and illusion. (How I Believe,* p. 33.)

It is, logically, a doctrine of passivity, of relaxation of tension, of withdrawal from things. A doctrine, in fact, that is totally ineffective and dead. It is precisely the *reverse* of what true human mysticism, born in the West, looks for if it is to be able to develop itself fully. For the western mystic the

unity that demands our worship is to be found at the term
not of a suppression or attenuation of the real but of an effort
of universal convergence. God is arrived at not in a negation,
but in an extension, of the world. (S.C., p. 106.)

Unlike the venerable cosmogonies of Asia which I have
just dismissed, the *humanist pantheisms* represent in our world
an extremely youthful form of religion. It is a religion which
(apart from Marxism) as yet knows little or no codification,
a religion with no apparent god, and with no revelation.
But it is religion in the true sense of the word, if by that
word we mean contagious faith in an ideal to which a man's
life can be given. In spite of many differences in detail, a
rapidly increasing number of our contemporaries is henceforth agreed in recognizing that the supreme value of life
consists in devoting oneself body and soul to universal
progress – this progress being expressed in the tangible
developments of mankind. It is a very long time since the
world has witnessed such an effect of 'conversion'. This,
surely, can only mean that in forms that vary (Communist
or nationalist, scientific or political, individual or collective)
we have without any doubt been watching for the last
century the birth and establishment of a new faith: the
religion of evolution. . . .

I rejected the East because it left no logical place or value
for the developments of nature. In humanisms, on the other
hand, I find the genesis of the greatest measure of consciousness, with its essential accompaniment of creation and research of every kind erected into a sort of absolute. In this
I see a stimulation to unlimited efforts to conquer time and
space. This, I feel, is the natural interior climate to develop
and evolve in which I am made. I can find no other explanation for the immediate sympathy and profound agreement

I have always noted between myself and the most emancipated servants of the earth. I have often been beguiled, accordingly, by dreams of venturing in their footsteps, curious to discover how far our paths might coincide. But on each occasion, I have very soon been disappointed. What I found was that after a fine start the worshippers of progress immediately come to a halt, without the desire or ability to go beyond the second stage in my individual belief. They set out eagerly, it is true, towards faith in spirit (the *true* spirit of sublimation and synthesis), but at the same time they hold back from investigating whether, to justify the gift they make of themselves, this spirit must be seen by them as endowed with immortality and personality. Much more often than not they deny it these two properties, which, in my view, are essential to the justification of man's effort; or, at any rate, they try to build up the body of their religion without reference to those properties. This very soon produces a feeling of insecurity, of incompleteness, and of suffocation.

The Hindu religions gave me the impression of a vast well into which one plunges in order to grasp the reflection of the sun. When I turn to the humanist pantheisms of today I feel that the lowering sky is pressing down on me and stifling me. (*How I Believe*, pp. 34–5.)

When, finally, we turn to *Christianity*, two observations must be made, one affirmative, one a restrictive qualification, if we are to cover the situation.

First, and most important, it is clear that by its very structure Christianity has always found its proper balance by directing itself towards the Spirit that unifies and synthesizes. God finally becomes *all in all* in an atmosphere of pure charity (*sola caritas*). That magnificent definition of the pantheism of differentiation expresses in unmistakable terms the very substance of Christ's message.

That, however, is far from meaning that, whether in its mystical expression or in its dogmatic formulation, the centric and centrifying character of the movement can yet be regarded as perfectly defined. . . .

Is it not obvious that Christianity will be able to breathe freely and spread its wings wide only if it can look forward in the end to the full realization of its spiritual potentialities, and that this calls for a true philosophy not simply of the Whole but of a convergent Whole?

The time has undoubtedly come when a new mysticism, at once fully human and Christian, must finally appear, at the opposite pole from an outworn orientalism: that is the road of the West, the road of tomorrow's World. (A.E. (*Oeuvres* VII), pp. 234-6.)

This Christian renaissance, which Teilhard called for with all his faith, is the subject of Chapter 5. The very dynamism of the 'Christian phylum', of which the Council provided a telling example, is an overpowering proof of the truth of Christianity.

First, however, we must see how this singular 'Christian phenomenon' can be described from without.

III. THE CHRISTIAN PHENOMENON

Historically, starting with the man Jesus Christ, a phylum of religious thought appeared within the human mass, and its presence has continually influenced more and more widely and deeply the development of the Noosphere. Nowhere, outside this remarkable current of consciousness, has the idea of God and the significant act of worship attained such clarity, such richness, such coherence and flexibility. And all this has been maintained and fed by the conviction that it is the answer to an inspiration and a revelation from on high. (A.E. (*Oeuvres* VII), p. 154.)

From the supremely realist and biological point of view adopted by Catholic dogma, the Universe represents:
(1) the arduous, personalizing, unification in God of a tenuous mass of souls which are distinct from God and at the same time in suspension from him; (2) by incorporation in Christ (incarnate God), (3) through the building up of the collective humano–Christian unit (the Church).

'When Christ has assimilated all things unto himself, then he will himself also be subject unto him who put all things under him, that God may be all in all.' (St Paul.)

From this it follows that a threefold faith is the essential and sufficient basis of the Christian attitude:

1. Faith in the Personality (the personalizing personality of God, the focus of the World).

2. Faith in the divinity of the historical Christ (not only as prophet and perfect man, but as an object also of love and worship).

3. Faith in the reality of the Church–*phylum* (in which, and centred on which, Christ continues to develop, in the World, his total personality). (*Introduction à la Vie chrétienne*, 1944, *Oeuvres* X, pp. 179–80.)

Since the Christian Universe consists, structurally, in the unification of elementary persons in a supreme Personality (which is God's), the ultimate dominating energy of the whole system can only be an interpersonal attraction: in other words it must be one of love.

In consequence, God's love for the world and for each of the elements of the world, and the love, too, that the elements of world have for one another and for God, are more than a secondary effect attached to the process of creation:

they represent also both its operative factor and its basic dynamism. (Ibid.)

In the first place, whatever may be said, a love – a *true* love – of God is perfectly possible. If it were not, all the monasteries and churches in the world would empty overnight; and Christianity, in spite of its framework of ritual, teaching and hierarchy, would inevitably collapse into nothingness.

Secondly, there is no doubt that this love finds greater strength in Christianity than anywhere else. If that were not so, then, in spite of all the excellences and all the appeal of the kindly Gospel teaching, the doctrine of the Beatitudes and of the Cross would long ago have been replaced by some Creed with more emphasis on mastery – and, more particularly, some form of humanism or what we might call 'terrenism'.

Whatever may be the merits of the other religions, it is an undeniable fact, explain it how you will, that the most ardent collective focus of love that has yet appeared in the world, burns here and now at the heart of God's Church. (*Le Christique*, unpublished, 1955.)

Must we not recognize, at the source of this mystical current that has such remarkable vitality, the creative flood at the peak of its intensity – the spark that leaps the gap between God and the Universe through a personal *milieu* – the message, precisely, which we were justified in expecting? (A.E. (*Oeuvres* VII), p. 154.)

IV. THE ACT OF FAITH

Here, indeed, is the crucial choice upon which everything

else depends. Just, in fact, as the refusal to recognize the organic value of the social fact would leave us (at the first stage of this dialectic) no reason to believe in an ultra-human extension of evolution, so now the refusal to recognize the Christian fact would mean that we saw the vault of the Universe, after momentarily opening out above us, again hermetically sealed.

On the other hand, if we take the step – if, that is to say, we are prepared (as reasonable probability suggests) to see in the living thought of the Church the reflection, adapted to our evolutionary condition, of the divine thought – then our spirit can resume its forward advance. And, if we make our way for a third time to the summit of all things we shall see it not simply as the centre of consistence, nor simply as a psychical prime mover, nor even simply as a being that addresses us, but as a Word that is incarnate. If, then, the Universe rises up progressively towards unity, this is not merely due to some external force; it is because the transcendent becomes to some degree immanent in it. There we have the lesson of Revelation.

At this point, however, before going any further, we should stop for a moment and note what is presupposed by the step we have just taken and what new contribution, also, it adds to the nature of our adherence. Hitherto we have advanced, in our looking forward to fuller being, only along the road of reason, each of our successive intuitions operating within the scientific framework of 'hypothesis'. From the moment we admit the reality of an answer that comes to us from on high, we in some way enter into the order of certainty. This, however, is effected only through a mechanism not simply of confrontation of subject with object but of contact between two centres of consciousness. It is no longer an act of cognition but of recognition; it is the complex interaction of two beings who freely open themselves and give themselves to one another – the emergence, under the influence of grace, of theological Faith. (A.E. (*Oeuvres* VII), pp. 154–5.)

4. The Living Church and Christ-Omega

I. THE LIVING CHURCH

Once the fact of the Incarnation has been recognized, we are in a position to appreciate more profoundly the nature of the Christian phenomenon. We see beyond the teaching Church to the living Church: the seed of super-vitalization planted in the Noosphere by the historical appearance of Christ Jesus. (A.E. (*Oeuvres* VII), p. 155.)

In this connection, we see an additional element beginning to take shape in the actual nucleus of the cone of cosmic involution. At first we had recognized that the central phenomenon in the Universe is Life: in Life it is Thought, and in Thought the collective arrangement of thoughts in interrelation to one another. We are now faced by a *fourth choice*, and it brings us to the conclusion that at a still deeper level, at the very heart, that is to say, of the social phenomenon, a sort of *ultra-socialization* is in progress. It is the process by which 'the Church' is gradually formed, its influence animating and assembling in their most sublime form all the spiritual energies of the Noosphere: the Church, the reflexively Christified portion of the world – the Church, the principal focus-point at which inter-human affinities come together through super-charity – the Church, the central axis of universal convergence, and the exact meeting-point that springs up between the Universe and Omega Point. (*Comment je vois*, para. 24.)

II. CHRIST-OMEGA

(Super-Christ, the Universal Christ, Christ the Evolver, the Cosmic Christ)

For ninety per cent of those who view him from outside, the Christian God looks like a great landowner administering his estates, the world. Now this conventional picture, which is too well justified by appearances, corresponds in no way to the dogmatic basis or point of view of the Gospels. And for this reason. The essence of Christianity is neither more nor less than a belief in the unification of the world in God by the Incarnation. All the rest is only secondary explanation or illustration. In view of this, so long as human society had not emerged from the 'neolithic', family phase of its development (that is to say until the dawn of the modern scientific-industrial phase) clearly the Incarnation could only find symbols of a juridical nature to express it. But since our modern discovery of the great unities and vast energies of the cosmos, the ancient words begin to assume a new and more satisfying meaning. To be the alpha and omega, Christ must, without losing his precise humanity, become co-extensive with the physical expanse of time and space. In order to reign on earth, he must 'super-animate' the world. In him henceforth, by the whole logic of Christianity, personality expands (or rather centres itself) till it becomes universal. Is this not exactly the God we are waiting for?

I will not go so far as to say that this religious renaissance is yet self-conscious. In all realms, the old framework resists hardest when it is at breaking-point. But my experience of Christianity allows me to affirm this: whatever formalisms may still persist, the transformation of which I speak has already taken place in the most living parts of the Christian organism. Beneath a surface pessimism, individualism or juridicism, Christ the King is *already worshipped today as the God of progress and evolution.* (H.E., pp. 91–2.)

By Super-Christ I most certainly do not mean *another* Christ, a second Christ different from and greater than the first. I mean *the same* Christ, the Christ of all time, revealing himself to us in a form and in dimensions, with an urgency and area of contact, that are enlarged and given new force.

We may dig things over as much as we please, but the Universe cannot have two heads. The universal Christic centre, determined by theology, and the universal cosmic centre postulated by anthropogenesis: these two focal points ultimately coincide (or at least overlap) in the historical setting in which we are contained. Christ would not be the sole Mover, the sole Issue, of the Universe if it were possible for the Universe in any way to integrate itself, even to a lesser degree, apart from Christ. And even more certainly, Christ, it would seem, would have been physically incapable of supernaturally centring the Universe upon himself if it had not provided the Incarnation with a specially favoured point at which, in virtue of their natural structure, all the strands of the cosmos tend to meet together. It is therefore towards Christ, in fact, that we turn our eyes when, however approximate our concept of it may be, we look ahead towards a higher pole of humanization and personalization.

In position and function, Christ, here and now, fills for us the place of Omega Point.

St Paul's boldest sayings readily take on a literal meaning as soon as the world is seen to be suspended, by its conscious side, from an Omega point of convergence, and Christ, in virtue of his Incarnation, is recognized as carrying out precisely the functions of Omega.

If Christ does indeed hold the position of Omega in the heaven of our Universe (and this is perfectly possible, since, structurally, Omega is super-personal in nature) then a whole series of remarkable properties become the prerogative of his risen Humanity.

In the first place, he is physically and literally, *He who fills all things*: at no instant in the world, is there any element of the world that has moved, that moves, that shall ever move outside the directing flood he pours into them. Space and duration are filled by him.

Again physically and literally, he is he who *consummates*: the plenitude of the world being finally effected only in the final synthesis in which a supreme consciousness will appear upon total, supremely organized, complexity. And since he, Christ, is the organic principle of this harmonizing process, the whole Universe is *ipso facto* stamped with his character, shaped according to his direction, and animated by his form.

Finally, and once more physically and literally, since all the structural lines of the world converge upon him and are knitted together in him, it is he who *gives its consistence* to the entire edifice of Matter and Spirit. In him too, '*the head of Creation*', it follows, the fundamental cosmic process of Cephalization culminates and is completed, on a scale that is universal and with a depth that is supernatural, and yet in harmony with the whole of the Past.

We see, then, that there is no exaggeration in using the term Super-Christ to express that excess of greatness assumed in our consciousness by the Person of Christ in step with the awakening of our minds to the super-dimensions of the world and of mankind.

It is not, I insist, another Christ, it is the same Christ, still and always the same, and even more so in that it is precisely in order to retain for him his essential property of being *co-extensive with the world* that we are obliged to make him undergo this colossal magnification.

Christ–Omega: the Christ, therefore, who animates and gathers up all the biological and spiritual energies developed by the Universe. Finally, then, Christ the evolver.

It is in that form, now clearly defined and all-embracing, that Christ the Redeemer and Saviour henceforth offers himself for our worship. (S.C., pp. 164–7.)

5. The Religion of Tomorrow

I. TOWARDS A CHRISTIAN REVIVAL

For almost all the ancient religions, the renewal of cosmic outlook characterizing 'the modern mind' has occasioned a crisis of such severity that, if they have not yet been killed by it, it is plain they will never recover. Narrowly bound to untenable myths, or steeped in a pessimistic and passive mysticism, they can adjust themselves neither to the precise immensities nor to the constructive requirements of space-time. They are out of step both with our science and with our activity.

But under the shock which is rapidly causing its rivals to disappear, Christianity, which might at first have been thought to be shaken too, is showing, on the contrary, every sign of forging ahead. For by the very fact of the new dimensions assumed by the universe as we see it today, it reveals itself both as inherently more vigorous in itself and as more necessary to the world than it has ever been before. (P.M., p. 296; Fontana, pp. 324–5.)

What is finally the most revolutionary and fruitful aspect of our present age is the relationship it has brought to light between matter and spirit: spirit being no longer independent of matter, or in opposition to it, but laboriously emerging from it under the attraction of God by way of synthesis and centration.

But what is the effect, for Christian faith and mysticism, of this redefinition of Spirit? It is simply to confer reality and absolute urgency upon the double dogma on which the whole of Christianity rests, and by which it is summed up:

the physical primacy of Christ and the moral primacy of charity. (F.M., pp. 93–4; Fontana, pp. 96–7.)

In this connection, see the preceding chapter, with its treatment of the universal dimensions of Christ-Omega and its definition of mysticism from the more inclusive angle of Super-charity.

Christianity, by its very essence, is much more than a fixed system, formulated once and for all, of truths that must be accepted and preserved literally. For all its basis in a nucleus of 'revelation', it constitutes in fact a spiritual attitude that is continually developing: it represents the development of a Christic consciousness that keeps pace with and is required by the growing consciousness of mankind. It behaves, biologically, like a phylum. By biological necessity, therefore, it must have the structure of a phylum; in other words it must form a coherent and progressive system of spiritual elements collectively associated.

Once that is accepted, it becomes clear that, here and now, nothing within Christianity except Catholicism possesses these characteristics.

There are, no doubt, numerous individuals outside Catholicism who see and love Christ and are therefore united to him as closely as Catholics (and even more closely). These, however, are not grouped together in the 'cephalized' unity of a body which reacts vitally, as an organic whole, to the combined forces of Christ and Humanity.

They are fed by the sap that flows in the trunk without sharing in its elaboration and in its youthful surge at the very heart of the tree. Experience is at hand to prove that this is so. Not only logically but as a matter of fact it is only in Catholicism that new dogmas continue to germinate – and, more widely, that those new attitudes are produced which, by a constant synthesis of the age-old Creed and the views newly emerged in man's consciousness, are preparing in our world of today the coming of a Christian humanism.

It is abundantly clear that if Christianity (as it professes and feels itself to be) is indeed destined to be the religion of tomorrow, it can only be through the living, organic, axis of its Roman Catholicism that it can hope to be a match for, and assimilate to itself, the great modern currents of humanitarianism.

To be Catholic is the only way of being fully and completely Christian. (*Introduction à la Vie chrétienne (Oeuvres* X), pp. 196-7.)

As soon as, indeed instead of isolating it and opposing it to what has motion, we resolutely 'plug it into' the forward moving world, Christianity – however worn out it may appear to our modern Gentiles – immediately and completely regains its original power of activating and attracting.

And this is because, of all the forms of worship produced in the course of man's history, only Christianity, once this 'connection' has been made, shows the astonishing power of energizing to the maximum, by 'amorizing', both the forces of growth and life and those of diminishment and death, within and during the Noogenesis in which we are involved.

It is still Christianity, I repeat, and Christianity it will always be: but it is a 're-born' Christianity, as certain of victory tomorrow as it was in its first days – because it alone (through the twofold virtue, *now at last understood in its total truth*, of its Cross and Resurrection) is capable of becoming the religion that provides the specific motive force for evolution. (*Le Christique*, unpublished.)

II. TOWARDS THE ABOVE THROUGH THE AHEAD

Without a 'convergent' view of the world, of which the Christian type is an example, the structure built up by human action is in danger of collapsing for lack of a keystone to set in the arch. (S.C., p. 108.)

It used to appear, with almost geometric certainty, that only two attitudes were possible for man: either loving heaven or loving the earth. With a new view of space, a third road opens up: to make our way to heaven through the earth. Communion (the *true* communion) with God can be attained through the world; and to adopt that road is not to take the impossible step of trying to serve two masters.

Such a Christianity is still in real fact the true application of the Gospel, since it represents the same force applied to the elevation of mankind, in a common love, above the tangible.

At the same time such evangelical teaching no longer smacks of the opium for dispensing which to the masses we are so bitterly (and with some justification) reproached.

Nor is it merely the soothing oil poured into the wounds – the lubricant for the labouring machinery – of mankind.

The truth is that it comes to us as the animator of human action, to which it offers the sharply defined ideal of a divine figure glimpsed in history, a figure in whom all that is essentially most precious in the Universe is concentrated and preserved.

It is the exact answer to all the doubts and aspirations of an age that has suddenly woken into consciousness of its future.

That teaching, and that alone, so far as we can judge, is showing itself capable of justifying and maintaining in the world the fundamental zest for life.

It is the very Religion of Evolution. (*Christologie et Évolution*, 1933 (*Oeuvres* X), pp. 111–12.)

To sum up, in order to match the new curve of time, Christianity is led to discover the values of this world *below the level of God*, while Humanism finds room for a God *above the level of this world*. Inverse and complementary movements: or rather, the two faces of a single event which perhaps marks the beginning of a new era for mankind.

This double transformation is something more than a speculation of my own. Throughout the world at this moment, without distinction of country, class, calling or creed, men are appearing who have begun to reason, to act and to pray, in terms of the limitless and organic dimensions of Space-time. To the outside observer, such men may still seem isolated. But they are aware of one another among themselves, they recognize each other whenever their paths cross. They know that tomorrow, rejecting old concepts, divisions and forms, the whole world will see what they see and think as they do. (F.M., p. 96, Fontana, pp. 99–100.)

Let there be revealed to us the possibility of believing *at the same time and wholly* in God *and* the world, the one through the other: let this belief burst forth, as it is ineluctably in process of doing under the pressure of those seemingly opposed forces, and then, we may be sure of it, a great flame will illumine all things: for a Faith will have been born (or reborn) containing and embracing all others – and inevitably it is the strongest Faith which sooner or later must possess the earth. (F.M., pp. 268–9; Fontana, p. 281.)

6. Revelation and the Christian Phenomenon

The likelihood of a reaction (or reflection) of Omega on the Human as the latter advances towards co-reflexion (Revelation and the Christian Phenomenon).

The more we consider the indispensability of an Omega to maintain and animate the continued progress of hominized Evolution, the more clearly can we see two things.

The first is that a purely conjectural Omega – one that was arrived at simply by 'calculation' – would be powerless to keep active in man's heart a passion strong enough to make him continue the process of hominization to the very end.

The second is that if Omega does really exist, it is difficult not to accept that its supreme 'Ego' in some way makes itself felt as such by all the imperfect Egos (that is to say all the reflective elements) of the Universe.

From this point of view the ancient and traditional idea of 'Revelation' reappears and again finds a place in Cosmogenesis – entering it, this time, through biology and the energetics of evolution.

From this point of view, again, the Christian mystical current takes on an extraordinary significance and actuality: and this because, while it is true that, by the logic of energetics, the heart of some intense faith is absolutely indispensable to the completion of the process of complexity-consciousness, at the same time it is equally true (how true, you have only to look around the world to realize) that at the present moment no faith can be distinguished that is capable of fully taking over (by 'amorizing' it) a convergent Cosmogenesis, except faith in a Christ, a Christ of the Pleroma and Parousia, *in quo omnia constant*, in whom all things find their consistence.

Part Three

Morality and Mysticism

1. Natural Morality

I. MORALITY

One of the most important aspects of hominization, from the point of view of the history of life, is the accession of biological realities (or values) to the domain of moral realities (or values).[1] (H.E., p. 29.)

Morality arose largely as an empirical defence of the individual and society. Ever since intelligent beings began to be in contact, and consequently in friction, they have felt the need to guard themselves against each other's encroachments. And once an arrangement was in practice discovered which more or less guaranteed to each one his due, this system itself felt the need to guarantee itself against the changes which would call its accepted solutions into question and disturb the established social order. (H.E., pp. 105–6.)

In the widest sense of the word, we may give the name of morality to every coherent system of action that is accepted by necessity or convention. In the strict sense it is a coherent system of action which must be *universal* (governing all human activity) and *categorical* (involving some form of obligation). (*La Morale peut-elle se passer de soubassements métaphysiques avoués ou inavoués*, unpublished, 1945.)

II. OBLIGATION

Act we must – but why and how?[2]

So long as our conceptions of the Universe remained

---

[1] See above, 'Human Energy', p. 57.
[2] Cf. The cosmic problem of action.

static, the basis of duty remained extremely obscure. To account for this mysterious law which weighs fundamentally on our liberty, men had recourse to all sorts of explanations, from that of an explicit command issued from outside to that of an irrational but categorical instinct. In a spiritually evolutionary scheme of the Universe, such as we have here accepted, the answer is quite simple. For the human unity, the *initial* basis of obligation is the fact of being born and developing *as a function of a cosmic stream*. We must act, and in a certain way, because our individual destinies are dependent on a universal destiny. *Duty, in its origin, is nothing but the reflection of the universe in the atom.* (H.E., p. 29. Last sentence italicized by editor.)

III. MORALITY OF MOVEMENT AND MORALIZATION

Morality has till now been principally understood as a fixed system of rights and duties intended to establish a static equilibrium between individuals, and at pains to maintain it by a *limitation* of energies, that is to say of force.

This conception rested in the last resort on the idea that every human being represented a sort of absolute term in the world, whose existence had to be protected from all encroachment from without. It is transformed from top to bottom if one recognizes, as we have just done, that man on earth is no more than an element destined to complete himself cosmically in a higher consciousness in process of formation. Now the problem confronting morality is no longer how to reserve and protect the individual but how to guide him so effectively in the direction of his anticipated fulfilments that the 'quantity of personality' still diffuse in humanity may be released in fullness and security. The moralist was up to now a jurist, or a tight-rope walker. He becomes the technician and engineer of the spiritual energies of the world. The highest morality is henceforth that which will best develop the phenomenon of nature to its upper limits. No longer to protect but to develop, by awakening and convergence, the individual riches of the earth. (H.E., p. 106.)

And thus we discover the new idea of a *moralization*, to be understood as the indefinitely continuous discovery and conquest of the animate powers of the Earth. To the morality of balance ('closed morality') the moral world might seem a definitely bounded realm. To the morality of movement ('open morality') the same world appears as a higher sphere of the universe, much richer than the lower spheres of matter in unknown powers and unsuspected combinations. The boldest mariners of tomorrow will sail out to explore and humanize the mysterious ocean of moral energies. (H.E., p. 108.)

V. THE SPIRITUAL FUNCTION OF GOD

A morality of balance can be constructed and subsist closed in on itself. Since it sets out only to adjust associated elements to one another, it is sufficiently determined and sustained by a mutual agreement of the parties it reconciles. A minimum of internal frictions in a regulated state is both the ideal to which it tends and a sign that it has reached it.

In the morality of movement, on the contrary, which is only defined by relation to a state or object to be reached, it is imperative that the goal shall shine with enough light to be desired and held in view. Examined in its external development, the phenomenon of spirit appeared to us to depend on a common centre of total organization. Observed now in its internal functioning, it brings us – as was inevitable – face to face with this pole of attraction and total determination.

A morality of balance may logically be agnostic and engrossed in possession of the present moment. A morality of movement necessarily inclines towards the future, in pursuit of a God. (H.E., pp. 108–9.)

In short, humanity has reached the biological point where it must either lose all belief in the universe or quite resolutely worship it. (Ibid, pp. 109–10.)

The definitive discovery of the phenomenon of spirit is accordingly bound up with the analysis (which science will one day finally undertake) of the 'mystical phenomenon', that is, of the love of God. (Ibid, p. 112.)

2. Mysticism

It is upon this Physics that Père Teilhard simultaneously builds up, secondly, a Mysticism:

The whole of Evolution being reduced to a process of union with God, it becomes, in its totality, loving and lovable in the innermost and most ultimate of its developments.

I. THE ORIGIN OF MYSTICISM: THE COSMIC SENSE

I give the name of cosmic sense to the more or less confused affinity that binds us psychologically to the All which envelops us. The existence of this feeling is indubitable, and apparently as old as the beginning of thought. . . .

The cosmic sense must have been born as soon as man found himself facing the forest, the sea and the stars. And since then we find evidence of it in all our experience of the great and unbounded: in art, in poetry, in religion. Through it we react to the world 'as a whole'[1] as with our eyes to light. (H.E., p. 82.)

At the psychological root of all mysticism there lies, if I am not mistaken, the more or less vague attraction or need that urges every conscious element to become one with the whole that encompasses it. This *cosmic* sense, which is undoubtedly akin to and as primordial as the sexual sense, but has intermittently been very active in certain poets or seers, has hitherto remained dormant or has at any rate been confined (in an elementary and questionable form) to some eastern centres. (*Comment je vois*, para. 35.)

[1] Père Teilhard uses the English phrase.

In this context I mean by mysticism the need, the science and the art of attaining the Universal and the Spiritual at the same time and each through the other. Simultaneously, and by the same significant act, to become one with All, through emancipation from all multiplicity or material gravity – that, deeper than any ambition for pleasure, wealth or power, is the essential cream of the human soul. It is a dream that as yet has been imperfectly or incompletely formulated in the Noosphere, but one that can clearly be distinguished throughout the whole of the already long history of Holiness. (Ibid., para. 32.)

II. TWO OPPOSED FORMS OF THE MYSTICAL SPIRIT.

An effort to escape spiritually, through universalization, into the inexpressible: mystics of all religions and of all times are in complete agreement about this general orientation of the interior life in search of perfection. But I have long been convinced that this superficial unanimity disguises a serious opposition (or even a fundamental incompatibility) which originates in a confusion between two symmetrical but 'antipodal' approaches to the understanding, and hence the pursuit of Unity of Spirit.

a. According to the first (to which I shall give the more or less conventional name of 'the road of the East') spiritual unification is conceived as being brought about through a return to a common 'divine' basis that *underlies* all the sensibly apprehended determined manifestations of the Universe, and is *more real* than they are. From this first point of view, mystical Unity appears and is attained through direct suppression of the Multiple, in other words through relaxation of the cosmic effort towards differentiation that is active in and around us. This is the pantheism of identification, the Spirit 'of release of tension'.

b. According to the second approach, on the contrary (the road of the West), it is impossible to become one with All without carrying to their extreme limit, in their simultaneous progress towards differentiation and convergence, the dispersed elements that constitute us and surround us. From this second point of view, the 'common basis' of the eastern approach is mere illusion: all that there is is a central focus to which we can make our way only if we extend the countless directive forces of the Universe to the point at which they meet. This is the pantheism of union (and so of love), the Spirit 'of tension'. . . .

Here, indeed, we have a paradox. Although these two attitudes are each the exact opposite of the other, it would appear that no clear distinction has yet been made between them. This accounts for the extreme confusion that runs together or identifies the Ineffable of the Vedanta with that of such mystics as St John of the Cross, and so not only allows countless numbers of excellent souls to become helpless victims of the most pernicious illusions that are produced in the East, but, what is much more serious, delays a task that is daily becoming more urgent – the individualization and the full flowering of a worthy and powerful modern Mysticism. (*Comment je vois*, para. 33.)

In recent times there has emerged in our interior vision a Universe that has at last become knit together around itself and around ourselves through the immensity of time and space. As a result, it is quite evident that the passionate awareness of a universal quasi-presence is tending to be aroused, to become correctly adjusted and to be generalized in human consciousness. The sense of Evolution, the sense of species, the sense of the Earth, the sense of Man: these are so many different and preliminary expressions of one and the same new thirst for unification – and, it goes without saying, they all, by establishing a correct relation to the object that gives rise to them and stimulates them, conform to the western type of spiritualization and worship. Contradicting the most obstinate of preconceived opinions, the Light is on the point of appearing not from the East but here at home, in the very heart and centre of Technology and Research. (*Comment je vois*, para. 35.)

At this point, Père Teilhard was in a position to return to the classification of religions that, in his apologetics, led up to the demonstration that, on the point of Faith and in what concerns our activity, only Christianity has the vocation to super-animate modern neo-humanism. To this he adds an appeal, to all who are willing to listen, urging the 'necessity to formulate as soon as possible a mysticism of the West'.

For centuries, Hindu mysticism of fusion and Christian mysticism of the 'juridical' type have been the object of countless descriptions and codifications; nevertheless it is impossible at this moment to find a single printed work that affirms the existence and describes the specific properties of an interior attitude (the centric cosmic sense) in which, through force of circumstances we are all, without it being openly apparent, beginning to live. Our generation cannot enter into an Ultra-human whose reality becomes every day more evident except with the assistance of a new form of psychic energy; in that energy the personalizing depth of love is combined with the totalization of all that is most essential and most universal in the stuff of the cosmic stream – and yet we have no name for it!

The time has undoubtedly come when a new mysticism,

at once fully human and Christian, must finally appear at the opposite pole from an outworn orientalism: the road of the West – the road of tomorrow's world. (A.E. (*Oeuvres* VII), p. 236.)

In a number of essays, Teilhard developed this mystical teaching of impassioned work accomplished in a Christic Faith, writing with precision and with a most authentic lyrical note. Among the most important are: Cosmic Life (1916); The Mystical Milieu (1917); The Priest (1918) (*in* Writings in Time of War); The Mass on the World (1923) (*in* Hymn of the Universe); Le Milieu Divin (1927) (*English translation 1960, Fontana Books, 1964*); Human Energy (1937) (*in* Human Energy); Le Cœur de la Matière (1950); Le Christique (1955). *The essence of this teaching follows in the next two sections and in the last chapter, which brings out the final sacrifice that is called for from our life, our work, and our love.*

III. SUPER-CHARITY

'To love (with a true love) the Universe in process of formation, in its totality and in its detail', 'to love evolution' – that is the paradoxical interior act that can immediately be effected in the Christic ambiance. (*Comment je vois*, para. 37.)

To say that Christ is the term and motive force of evolution, to say that he manifests himself as 'evolver', is implicitly to recognize that he becomes attainable in and through the whole process of evolution. Let us examine the consequences for our interior life of this amazing situation.

There are three, and they may be expressed as follows: 'Under the influence of the Super-Christ, our charity is universalized, becomes dynamic and is synthesized.'

Let us look at each of the terms of this threefold transformation in turn.

1. *First, our charity is universalized.* By definition, the Christian is and always has been, the man who loves God, and his neighbour as himself. But has not this love necessarily remained hitherto particularist and extrinsic in its explicit realization? For many who believe, Christ is still the mysterious personage who after having passed through history two thousand years ago now reigns in a heaven that is divorced from earth; and our neighbour is still a swarm of human individuals, multiplied with no recognizable rule or reason, and associated together by the arbitrary force of law and convention. In such a view there is little or even no place for the immensities of sidereal or animate matter, for the multitude of the world's natural elements and events, for the impressive unfolding of cosmic processes.

Now, it is precisely this pluralism, emotionally so confusing, which vanishes under the rays of the Super-Christ, to make way for a warm and resplendent unity.

Since, in fact, everything in the Universe ultimately proceeds towards Christ-Omega; since the whole of Cosmogenesis is ultimately, through Anthropogenesis, expressed in a Christogenesis, it follows that, in the integral totality of its tangible strata, the Real is charged with a divine Presence. As the mystics felt instinctively, everything becomes physically and literally lovable in God; and God, in return, becomes intelligible and lovable in everything around us. In the breadth and depth of its cosmic stuff, in the bewildering number of the elements and events that make it up, and in the wide sweep, too, of the overall currents that dominate it and carry it along as one single great river, the world, filled by God, appears to our enlightened eyes as simply a setting in which universal communion can be attained and a concrete expression of that communion.

2. *Secondly, our charity is energized.* Hitherto, to love God and one's neighbour might have seemed no more than an attitude of contemplation and compassion. Was not to love God to rise above human distractions and passions in order to find rest in the light and unvarying warmth of the divine Sun? And was not to love one's neighbour primarily to bind up the wounds of one's fellow-men and alleviate their suffering? Detachment and pity – escape from the world and mitigation of evil – in the eyes of the Gentiles could not those two notes be legitimately regarded as the Christian characteristics of Charity?

Here again we find a complete change: our whole outlook widens and is vitalized to the scale of the universalized Christ.

If, let me repeat, the whole progress of the world does indeed conform to a Christogenesis (or, which comes to the same thing, if Christ can be fully attained only at the term and peak of cosmic evolution) then it is abundantly clear that we can make our way towards him and apprehend him only in the effort to complete and synthesize everything in him. In consequence, it is the general ascent of life towards fuller consciousness, it is man's effort in its entirety, that are now organically and with full justification once more included among the things with which charity is concerned and which it hopes to achieve. If we are to love the Super-Christ we must at all costs see to it that the Universe and mankind push ahead, in us and in each of our co-elements – in particular in the other 'grains of thought', our fellow-men.

To co-operate in total cosmic evolution is the only act that can adequately express our devotion to an evolutive and universal Christ.

3. *By that very fact, our charity is synthesized.* At first that expression may seem obscure, and it should be explained.

In the detail, and on the scale of 'ordinary' life, much that we do is independent of love. To love (between 'persons') is to be drawn together and brought closer *centre-to-centre*. In our lives, the 'centric' condition is seldom achieved. It may be that we are dealing with objects (material, at a lower level than the living, or intellectual) which are by their nature non-centred and impersonal; it may be that in our human inter-relationships we come into contact with our fellows only 'tangentially', through our interests, through our functions, or for business dealings – in either case, we are generally working, or seeking, enjoying ourselves or suffering, without loving – without even suspecting that it is possible for us to love – the thing or person with which we are concerned. Thus our interior life remains fragmented and pluralized.

Consider, on the other hand, what happens if above (or rather at the heart of) this plurality there rises the central reality of Christ the Evolver. In virtue of his position at the Omega of the World, Christ, we have seen, represents the focus-point towards which and in which all things *converge*. In other words, he appears as a Person with whom all reality (provided we understand that in the appropriate positive sense) effects an approach and a contact in the only direction that is possible: *the line in which their centres lie*.

This can mean but one thing, that every operation, once it is directed towards him, assumes, without any change of its own nature, the psychical character of a centre-to-centre relationship, in other words, of an act of love.

Eating, drinking, working, seeking; creating truth or beauty or happiness; all these things could, until now, have seemed to us heterogeneous, disparate activities incapable of being reduced to terms of one another – loving being no more than one of a number of branches in this divergent psychical efflorescence.

Now, however, that it is directed towards the Super-Christ, the fascicle draws itself together. Like the countless shades that combine in nature to produce a single white light, so the infinite modalities of action are fused in one single colour under the mighty power of the universal Christ; and it is love that heads this movement: love, not simply the common factor through which the multiplicity of human activities attains its cohesion, but love, the *higher, universal, and synthesized form of spiritual energy*, in which all the other energies of the soul are transformed and sublimated, once they fall within 'the field of Omega'.

Originally, the Christian had no desire except to be able to love, at all times and whatever he was doing, *at the same time as he was acting*. Now he sees that he can love *by his activity*, in other words he can directly be united to the divine centre by his very action, no matter what form it may take.

In that centre, if I may use the phrase, every activity is 'amorized'. (S.C., pp. 167–71.)

IV. CHRISTIAN ASCESIS: ATTACHMENT AND DETACHMENT

The law and the ideal of all good (whether moral or physical) are expressed in a single rule (which is also a hope): 'in all things to work for, and accept, the organic unity of the world.' To work for it, in as much as it requires for its consummation the co-operation of its elements: to accept it, in as much as its realization is primarily the effect of a synthetic domination, superior to our own power. Confirmed, exactly defined, and transfigured by faith in the Incarnation, this rule of action takes on incomparable urgency and delightfulness: and it is readily expressed, too, in any number of immediate and practical obligations. We shall see that for the Christian who is dedicated to the unification of the world in Christ, the whole task of the interior moral and mystical life may be reduced to two essential and complementary processes: to conquer the world, and to escape from it. Each is a natural consequence of the other, and they represent two allied forms of one and the same urge: to come together with God through the world. (S.C., p. 66.)

a. *The Conquest of the World*

Every process of material growth in the Universe is ultimately directed towards spirit, and every process of spiritual growth is ultimately directed towards Christ. From this it follows that whether the work to which I am tied by the circumstances of the present moment be commonplace or sublime, tedious or enthralling, I have the happiness of being able to think that Christ is waiting to receive its fruit: and that fruit, we must remember, is not only the intention behind my action but also the tangible result of my work. '*Opus ipsum, et non tantum operatio*', the work itself and not simply its doing.

If this hope is justified, the Christian must be active, and busily active, working as earnestly as the most convinced of those who work to build up the earth, that Christ may continually be born more fully in the world around him. More than any unbeliever, he must respect and seek to advance human effort – effort in all its forms – and above all the human effort which is aimed more directly at increasing the consciousness (that is, the being) of mankind; by that I mean the scientific quest for truth, and the organized attempt to develop a better social nexus. In those aims, those who love the universal Christ should never let themselves be out-stripped in hope and boldness. No one, in fact, has so many reasons as they have for believing in the universe, and for launching an assault upon it in order to make it their own. (S.C., p. 68.)

May the time come when men, having been awakened to a sense of the close bond linking all the movements of this world in the single all-embracing work of the Incarnation, shall be unable to give themselves to any one of their tasks without illuminating it with the clear vision that their work – however elementary it may be – is received and put to good use by a divine Centre of the Universe.

When that comes to pass, there will be little to separate the life of the cloister from the life of the world. And only then will the action of the children of heaven (at the same time as the action of the children of the world) have attained the required plenitude of its humanity. (M.D., p. 40; Fontana, p. 67.)

b. *Detachment from the World*

1. *By action*

Nothing is more excruciating than effort, and that is true of spiritual effort too. If you ask the masters of the ascetical life what is the first, the most certain, and the most sublime of mortifications, they will all give you the same answer: it is the work of interior development by which we tear ourselves away from ourselves, leave ourselves behind, emerge from ourselves. Every individual life, if lived loyally, is strewn with the outer shells discarded by our successive metamorphoses – and the entire Universe leaves behind it a long series of states in which it might well have been pleased to linger with delight, but from which it has continually been torn away by the inexorable necessity to grow greater. This ascent in a continual sloughing off of the old is indeed a way of the Cross. (S.C., p. 69.)

2. *By passivity*

It is an infinite delight, no doubt, to the Christian, to grow greater for Christ (and the more so in that it is Christ himself, in the very depths of our being, who seeks to be born and grow greater in our bodies and souls: our ardour, our zest for life, is itself, indeed, a passivity). But this growth has ultimately no meaning or value except in so far as it allows us to provide the divine contact with a firmer grip. It is that contact we now have to effect. Where shall we find it? Is it, as we no doubt wonder, mysterious, infrequent, grudging, distant? If we are to offer ourselves to it, must we make our way into some area far above us on some extremely deep zone? The reality is much simpler and lovelier than we imagine.

'*In eo vivimus, movemur, et sumus*' – in him we live and move and have our being (St Paul). Christ operates, he exerts his living pressure, on the believer who can act and believe rightly, through all the surface and depth of the world. It is he who encompasses us and moulds us, at every moment, through all the passivities and restrictions of our lives.

This is the most magnificent of the prerogatives of the Universal Christ: the power to be operative in us, not only through the natural impulses of life but also through the shocking disorders of defeat and death.

This wonderful transformation, let me insist, is not effected immediately or without our co-operation. We are justified in resigning ourselves to evil only when we have first resisted it with all the strength at our command. *If we are to succeed in submitting ourselves to the will of God, we must first make a very great effort.* God is not to be found indiscriminately in the things that thwart us in life or the trials we have to suffer – but solely *at the point of balance* between our desperate efforts to grow greater and the resistance to our domination that we meet from outside. In that area of equilibrium, moreover, he is born only *in so far as we believe* that he is: 'Diligentibus, *omnia convertuntur in bonum*' – *for those who love,* all things are transformed into good.

. . . The world can attain God, in Jesus Christ, only by a complete recasting in which it must *appear* to be entirely lost, *with nothing* (of the terrestrial order) *that our experience could recognize as compensation.* When such a death, whether it be slow or rapid, takes place in us, we must open our hearts wide to the hope of union: never, if we so will it, will the animating power of the word have mastered us so fully. (S.C., pp. 71–3.)

It was a joy to me, O God, in the midst of the struggle, to feel that in developing myself I was increasing the hold that you had upon me; it was a joy to me, too, under the inner thrust of life or amid the favourable play of events, to abandon myself to your Providence. Now that I have found the joy of utilizing all forms of growth to make you, or to let you, grow in me, grant that I may without distress attain this last phase of communion in the course of which I shall possess you by diminishing in you.

After having perceived you as he who is 'a greater myself', grant, *when my hour comes,* that I may recognize you under the species of each alien or hostile force that seems bent upon destroying or uprooting me. When the signs of age begin to mark my body (and still more when they touch my mind); when the ill that is to diminish me or carry me off strikes from without or is born within me; when the painful moment comes in which I suddenly awaken to the fact that I I feel I am losing hold of myself and am absolutely passive in the hands of the great unknown forces that have formed me; in all those dark moments, grant, O God, that I may understand that it is you (provided only my faith is strong enough) who are painfully parting the fibres of my being in order to penetrate to the very marrow of my substance and bear me away within yourself.

The more deeply and incurably the evil is incrusted in my flesh, the more it will be you that I am harbouring – you as a loving, active principle of purification and detachment. The more the future opens before me like some dizzy abyss or dark tunnel, the more confident I may be – if I venture forward on the strength of your word – of losing myself and surrendering myself in you, of being assimilated by your body, Jesus. (M.D., pp. 69–70; Fontana, pp. 89–90.)

3. The Consummation of Mysticism

The *Milieu Divin* and *The Mass on the World*

1. WHAT IS THE DIVINE MILIEU?

a. *An ambience*

Action and acceptance: these two halves of our life – this inhaling and exhaling of our nature – are transfigured and clarified for us in the rays of creative union. Whatever we do, it is to Christ we do it. Whatever is done to us, it is Christ who does it. Christian piety has always drawn strength from these words of universal and constant union; but has it, I wonder, always been able, or been bold enough, to give to that union the forceful realism that, since St Paul first wrote these words, we have been entitled to expect?

Once we make up our minds to take the words of Revelation literally – and to do so is the ideal of all true religion – then the whole mass of the Universe is gradually bathed in light. And just as science shows us, at the lower limits of matter, an ethereal fluid in which everything is immersed and from which everything emerges, so at the upper limits of Spirit a mystical ambience appears in which everything floats and everything converges.

And in this rich and living ambience, the attributes, seemingly the most contradictory, of attachment and detachment, of action and contemplation, of the one and the multiple, of spirit and matter, are reconciled without difficulty in conformity with the designs of creative union: everything becomes one by becoming self. (S.C., pp. 73–4.)

Incomparably near and perceptible – for it presses in upon us through all the forces of the Universe – it nevertheless eludes our grasp so constantly that we can never seize it here below except by raising ourselves, uplifted on its waves, to the extreme limit of our effort: present in, and drawing at the inaccessible depth of each creature, it withdraws always further, bearing us along with it towards the common centre of all consummation.

Through it, the touch of matter is a purification, and chastity flowers as the transfiguration of love.

In it, development culminates in renunciation; attachment to things at the same time separates us from everything in them that is subject to decay. Death becomes a resurrection. (M.D., pp. 100–1; Fontana, p. 113.)

b. *A centre of convergence*

For all its vastness, the divine Milieu is in reality a *Centre*. It therefore has the properties of a centre, and above all the absolute and final power to unite (and consequently to complete) all beings in its embrace.

In the divine Milieu all the elements of the Universe *touch each other* by that which is most inward and ultimate in them. There they concentrate, little by little, all that is purest and most attractive in them without loss and without danger of subsequent corruption. There they shed, in their meeting, the mutual externality and the incoherences which form the basic pain of human relationships. Let those seek refuge there who are saddened by the separations, the meanness and the wastefulness of the world. In the external spheres of the world, man is always torn by the separations which set distance between bodies, which set the impossibility of mutual understanding between souls, which set death between lives. Moreover, at every minute he must lament that he cannot pursue and embrace everything within the compass of a few years. Finally, and not without reason, he is incessantly distressed by the crazy indifference and the heartbreaking dullness of a natural environment in which the greater part of individual endeavour seems wasted or lost, where the blow and the cry seem stifled on the spot, without awakening any echo. . . .

Let us establish ourselves in the divine Milieu. There we shall find ourselves where souls attain the fullness of their intimate essence. There we shall discover, where all beauties flow together, the ultra-vital, the ultra-sensitive, the ultra-active point of the Universe. And at the same time, we shall feel the *plenitude* of our powers of action and adoration effortlessly ordered within our deepest selves. (M.D., pp. 102–3; Fontana, pp. 114–15.)

If any words could express that permanent and lucid intoxication better than others, perhaps they would be 'passionate indifference'.

To have access to the divine Milieu is to have found the one thing needful: *him who burns* by setting fire to everything that we would love badly or not enough; *him who calms* by eclipsing with his blaze everything that has been snatched from our love or has never been given to it. To reach those priceless layers is to experience, with equal truth, that one has need of everything, and that one has need of nothing. Everything is needed, because the world will never be large enough to provide our zest for action with the means of grasping God, our thirst for acceptance with the possibility of being invaded by him. And yet nothing is needed: for, since the only reality that can satisfy us lies beyond the transparencies in which it is mirrored, the disappearance of all the corruptible that lies between that reality and ourselves can only have the effect of giving it back to us in a purer form. Everything means both everything and nothing to me; everything is God to me, and everything is dust to me; that is what man can say with equal truth, according to the direction in which the divine ray falls. (M.D., pp. 108–9; Fontana, p. 120.)

c. *A person*

The divine Milieu henceforward assumes for us the savour and the specific features which we desire. In it we recognize an omni-presence which acts upon us by assimilating us to itself, *in unitate corporis Christi* – in the unity of the body of Christ. As a consequence of the Incarnation, the divine immensity has transformed itself for us into *the omni-presence of Christification*. All the good that I can do – *opus et operatio* – is physically gathered, by something of itself, into the reality of the consummated Christ. Everything I endure, with faith and love, by way of diminishment or death, makes me a little more closely an integral part of his mystical body. Quite specifically it is *Christ whom we make or whom we undergo in all things*. (M.D., p. 112; Fontana, p. 123.)

Sometimes, when I have scrutinized the world very closely I have thought that I could see it enveloped in an atmosphere – still very tenuous but already individualized – of mutual good will and of truths accepted in common and retained as a permanent heritage. I have seen a shadow floating, as though it were the wraith of a universal soul seeking to be born. . . .

What name can we give to this mysterious Entity, who is in some small way our own handiwork, with whom, eminently, we can enter into communion; who is some part of ourselves, yet who masters us, has need of us in order to exist, and at the same time dominates us with the full force of his Absolute being?

I can feel it: he has a name and a face, but he alone can reveal his face and pronounce his name:

Jesus!

Together with all the beings around me I felt that I was caught up in a higher movement that was stirring together all the elements of the Universe and grouping them in a new order. When it was given to me to see where the dazzling trail of particular beauties and partial harmonies was leading, I recognized that it was all coming to centre *on a single point*, on a Person: your Person . . .

Jesus! (W.T.W., pp. 145–6.)

Tear away, O Jesus, the clouds with your lightning! Show yourself to us as the Mighty, the Radiant, the Risen! Come to us as the Pantocrator who reigned alone in the cupolas of the ancient basilicas. Nothing less than this Parousia is needed to counterbalance and dominate in our hearts the glory of the world that is coming into view. And so that we may triumph over the world with you, come to us clothed in the glory of the world. (M.D., p. 118; Fontana, p. 128.)

11. HOW CAN WE BECOME AT HOME IN THE DIVINE MILIEU?

a. *Prayer to the Holy Spirit*

The perception of the divine omnipresence is essentially a seeing, a taste, that is to say a sort of intuition bearing upon certain higher qualities in things. It cannot, therefore, be attained by any process of reasoning or any human artifice. It is a gift, like life itself, of which it is undoubtedly the supreme experiential perfection . . . to experience the attraction of God, to be sensible of the beauty, the consistence and the final unity of being, is the highest and at the same time the most complete of our 'passivities of growth'. God tends, by the logic of his creative effort, to make himself sought and perceived by us: '*Posuit homines . . . si forte attrectent eum*' – he made men . . . that they might grope their way towards him.

His prevenient grace is therefore always on the alert to excite our first look and our first prayer. But in the end the initiative, the awakening, always comes from him, and whatever the further developments of our mystical faculties, no progress is achieved in this domain except as the new response to a new gift. '*Nemo venit ad me, nisi Pater traxerit eum*' – no man can come to me unless the Father draws him.

We are thus led to posit intense and continual prayer at the origin of our invasion by the divine Milieu, the prayer which begs for the fundamental gift: '*Domine, fac ut videam*' – Lord, grant that I may see. Lord, we know and feel that you are everywhere around us, but it seems that there is a veil before our eyes. '*Illumina vultum tuum super nos*' – let the light of your countenance shine upon us in its universality. '*Sit splendor Domini nostri super nos*' – may your deep brilliance light up the innermost parts of the massive obscurities in which we move. And to that end, send us your Spirit, '*Spiritus principalis*,' whose flaming action alone can operate the birth and completion of the great metamorphosis that sums up all inward perfection and towards which your creation yearns: '*Emitte Spiritum tuum, et creabuntur, et renovabis faciem terrae*' – send forth thy Spirit and they shall be created: and thou shalt renew the face of the Earth. (M.D., pp. 122–3; Fontana, pp. 131–2.)

b. *Purity: Faith: Fidelity*

It could be said that three virtues contribute with particular effectiveness towards the limitless concentration of the divine in our lives – purity, faith, and fidelity. Under the converging action of these three rays, the world melts and folds.

Like a raging fire that is fed by what should normally extinguish it, or like a mighty torrent that is swelled by the very obstacles placed to stem it, so the tension engendered by the encounter between man and God dissolves, bears along and volatilizes created things, and makes them all, equally, serve the cause of union.

Joys, advances, sufferings, setbacks, mistakes, works, prayers, beauties, the powers of heaven, earth and hell – everything bows down under the touch of the heavenly waves; and everything yields up the portion of positive energy contained within its nature in order to contribute to the richness of the divine Milieu.

Like the jet of flame that effortlessly pierces the hardest

metal, so the spirit drawn to God penetrates through the world and makes its way enveloped in the luminous vapours of what it sublimates with him.

It does not destroy things or distort them; but it liberates things, directs them, transfigures them, animates them. It does not leave things behind but, as it rises, it leans on them for support; and carries along with it the chosen part of things.

Purity, faith and fidelity, static virtues and operative virtues, you are truly, in your serenity, nature's noblest energies – those which give even the material world its final consistency and ultimate shape. You are the formative principles of the New Earth. Through you, threefold aspect of one and the same trusting adoration, 'we overcome the world'. '*Haec est quae vincit Mundum, fides nostra*' – It is this that overcomes the world, our faith. (M.D., pp. 132–3; Fontana, p. 139.)

Fold your wings, my soul, those wings you had spread wide to soar to the terrestrial peaks where the light is most ardent. It is for you simply to await the descent of the Fire – supposing it to be willing to take possession of you.

If you are to attract its power to yourself, you must first loosen the bonds of affection which still tie you to objects cherished too exclusively for their own sake. The true union that you ought to seek with creatures that attract you is to be found not by going directly to them but by converging with them on God, sought in and through them. It is not by making themselves more material, relying solely on physical contacts, but by making themselves more spiritual in the embrace of God, that things draw closer to each other and, following their invincible natural bent, end by becoming, all of them together, one. Therefore, my soul, be chaste.

And when you have thus relieved your being of its burden of crude accretions, you must loosen yet further the fibres of your substance. In your excessive self-love you are like a molecule closed in upon itself and incapable of entering easily into any new combination. God looks to you to be more open and more pliant. If you are to enter into him you need to be freer and more eager. Have done, then, with your egoism and your fear of suffering. Love others as you love yourself, that is to say admit them into yourself, all of them, even those whom, if you were a pagan you would exclude. Accept pain. Take up your cross, my soul. (W.T.W.. pp. 143-4.)

III. THE TOTAL DIVINE MILIEU: THE COMMUNION OF SAINTS

The divine Milieu which will ultimately be one in the Pleroma, must begin to become one during the earthly phase of our existence. So that although the Christian who hungers to live in God may have attained all possible purity of desire, faith in prayer, and fidelity in action, the divinization of his universe is still open to vast possibilities. It would still remain for him to link his elementary work to that of all the labourers who surround him. The innumerable partial worlds which envelop the diverse human monads press in upon him from all around. His task is to re-kindle his own ardour by contact with the ardour of all these foci, to make his own sap communicate with that circulating in the other cells, to receive or propagate movement and life for the common benefit, and to adapt himself to the common temperature and tension.

The man with a passionate sense of the divine Milieu

cannot bear to find things about him obscure, tepid and empty which should be full and vibrant with God. He feels as though chilled to the bone by the thought of the numberless spirits which are linked to his in the unity of the same world, but are not yet fully kindled by the flame of the divine presence. He had thought for a time that he had only to stretch out his *own* hand in order to touch God to the measure of his desires. He now sees that the only human embrace capable of worthily enfolding the divine is that of all men opening their arms to call down and welcome the Fire. The only subject ultimately capable of mystical transfiguration is the whole group of mankind forming a single body and a single soul in Charity.

And this coalescence of the spiritual units of creation under the attraction of Christ is the supreme victory of faith over the world.

Jesus, Saviour of human activity to which you have given meaning, Saviour of human suffering to which you have given living value, be also the Saviour of human unity, compel us to discard our pettinesses, and to venture forth, resting upon you, into the uncharted ocean of charity. (M.D. pp. 136–7, 137–8, 140; Fontana, pp. 143, 144–5, 146.)

IV. MASS ON THE WORLD: COMMUNICATON WITH THE RISEN CHRIST

In spite of the strength of St Paul's expressions (formulated, it should be remembered, for the ordinary run of the first Christians) some readers may feel that we have been led to strain, in too realist a direction, the meaning of 'mystical body' – or at least that we have allowed ourselves to seek esoteric perspectives in it. But if we look a little more closely, we shall see that we have simply taken another path in order to rejoin the great highway opened up in the Church by the onrush of the cult of the Holy Eucharist.

When the priest says the words '*Hoc est Corpus meum*', his words fall directly on to the bread and directly transform it into the individual reality of Christ. But the great sacramental operation does not cease at that local and momentary event. Even children are taught that, throughout the life of each man and the life of the Church and the history of the world, there is only one Mass and one Communion. Christ died once in agony. Peter and Paul receive communion on such and such a day at a particular hour. But these different acts are only the diversely central points in which the continuity of a unique act is split up and fixed, in space and time, for our experience. In fact, from the beginning of the Messianic preparation, up till the Parousia, passing through the historic manifestation of Jesus and the phases of growth of his Church, a single event has been developing in the world: the Incarnation, realized, in each individual, through the Eucharist.

All the communions of a lifetime are one communion.

All the communions of all men now living are one communion

All the communions of all men, present, past and future, are one communion.

Have we ever sufficiently considered the physical immensity of man, and his extraordinary relations with the Universe, in order to realize in our minds the formidable implications of this elementary truth? (M.D., pp. 112–13; Fontana, pp. 123–4.)

Grant, O God, that when I draw near to the altar to communicate, I may henceforth discern the infinite perspectives hidden beneath the smallness and the nearness of the Host in which you are concealed. I have already accustomed myself to seeing, beneath the stillness of that piece of bread, a devouring power which, in the words of the greatest doctors of your Church, far from being consumed by me, consumes me. Give me the strength to rise above the remaining illusions which tend to make me think of your touch as circumscribed and momentary.

I am beginning to understand: under the sacramental Species it is primarily through the 'accidents' of matter that you touch me, but, as a consequence, it is also through the whole Universe in proportion as this ebbs and flows over me under your primary influence. In a true sense the arms and the heart which you open to me are nothing less than all the united powers of the world which, penetrated and permeated to their depths by your will, your tastes and your temperament, converge upon my being to form it, nourish it and bear it along towards the blazing centre of your fire. In the Host it is my life that you are offering me, O Jesus. (M.D., pp. 115–16; Fontana, p. 126.)

First of all I shall stretch out my hand unhesitatingly towards the fiery bread which you set before me. This bread, in which you have planted the seed of all that is to develop in the future, I recognize as containing the source and the secret of that destiny you have chosen for me. To take it is, I know, to surrender myself to forces which will tear me away painfully from myself in order to drive me into danger, into laborious undertakings, into a constant renewal of ideas, into an austere detachment where my affections are concerned. To eat it is to acquire a taste and an affinity for that which in everything is above everything – a taste and an affinity which will henceforward make impossible for me all the joys by which my life has been warmed. Lord Jesus, I am willing to be possessed by you, to be bound to your body and led by its inexpressible power towards those solitary heights which by myself I should never dare to climb. Instinctively, like all mankind, I would rather set up my tent here below on some hill-top of my own choosing. I am afraid, too, like all my fellow-men, of the future too heavy with mystery and too wholly new, towards which time is driving me. Then like these men I wonder anxiously where life is leading me . . . May this communion of bread with the Christ clothed in the powers which dilate the world free me from my timidities and my heedlessness! In the whirl-pool of conflicts and energies out of which must develop my power to apprehend and experience your holy presence, I throw myself, my God, on your word. The man who is filled with an impassioned love of Jesus hidden in the forces which bring increase to the earth, him the earth will lift up, like a mother, in the immensity of her arms, and will enable him to contemplate the face of God.

If your Kingdom, my God, were of this world, I could possess you simply by surrendering myself to the forces which cause us, through suffering and dying, to grow visibly in stature – us or that which is dearer to us than ourselves. But because the term towards which the earth is moving lies not merely beyond each individual thing but beyond the totality of things; because the world travails, not to bring forth from within itself some supreme reality, but to find its consummation through a union with a pre-existent Being, it follows that man can never reach a blazing centre of the universe simply by living more and more for himself or even by spending his life in the service of some earthly cause however great. The world can never be definitively united with you, Lord, save by a sort of reversal, a turning about, an *excentration*, which must involve the temporary collapse not merely of all individual achievements but even of everything that looks like an advancement for humanity. If my being is ever to be decisively attached to yours, there must first die in me not merely the monad ego but also the world: in other words I must first pass through an agonizing phase of diminution for which no tangible compensation will be given me. That is why, pouring into my chalice the bitterness of all separation, of all limitations, and of all sterile fallings away, you then hold it out to me. 'Drink ye all of this.'

How could I refuse this chalice, Lord, now that through the bread you have given me there has crept into the marrow of my being an inextinguishable longing to be united with you beyond life: through death?

My God, I deliver myself up with utter abandon to those fearful forces of dissolution which, I blindly believe, will this day cause my narrow ego to be replaced by your divine presence. The man who is filled with an impassioned love for Jesus hidden in the forces which bring death to the earth, him the earth will clasp in the immensity of her arms as her strength fails, and with her he will awaken in the bosom of God. (H. U., pp. 29–32.)

You are the irresistible and vivifying force, O Lord, and because yours is the energy, because, of the two of us, you are infinitely the stronger, it is on you that falls the part of consuming me in the union that should weld us together. Vouchsafe, therefore, something more precious still than the grace for which all the faithful pray. It is not enough that I should die while communicating. Teach me to treat my death as an act of communion. (M.D., p. 70; Fontana, p. 90.)

Conclusion

My intellectual position
(written in answer to a
questionnaire but never published).

The thought of Père Teilhard de Chardin in his own words: 'My intellectual position'.[1]

In its essence, the thought of Père Teilhard de Chardin is expressed not in a metaphysics but in a sort of phenomenology.

A certain law of recurrence, underlying and dominating all experience, he thinks, forces itself on our attention. It is the law of complexity-consciousness, by which, within life, the stuff of the cosmos folds in upon itself continually more closely, following a process of organization whose measure is a corresponding increase of tension (or psychic temperature). In the field of our observation, *reflective* man represents the highest term attained by an element in this process of organization.

Above individual man, however, this involution is carried further, in mankind, by the social phenomenon, at the term of which can be discerned a higher critical point of collective reflection.

From this point of view 'hominization' (including socialization) is a convergent phenomenon: in other words it displays an upper limit or internal point of maturity. At the same time this *convergent* phenomenon is also, in virtue of its structure, *irreversible* in nature: in this sense, that Evolution having become reflective and free, in man, it can no longer continue its ascent towards complexity-consciousness unless it realizes two things about 'vital involution' – that, looking

[1] In the pages that follow we give, as a continuous whole, the paper written by Père Teilhard in 1948 (see Introduction), passages from which have been given at the head of the preceding chapters.

145

ahead, it escapes annihilation or total death, and, what is more, that it gathers together all that can be permanently saved of the essence of what life will have engendered in the course of its progress. This demand for irreversibility has a structural implication, the existence, at the upper term of cosmic convergence, of a transcendent centre of unification, 'Omega Point'. Unless this focus-point, which gathers things together and ensures their irreversibility, does in fact exist, the law of evolutionary recurrence cannot hold good to the very end.

It is upon this 'Physics' that, in a 'second phase', Père Teilhard builds first an apologetics: under the illuminating influence of Grace, our minds recognize in the unifying properties of the Christian phenomenon a manifestation (or a reflection) of Omega upon human consciousness, and so identify the Omega of reason with the Universal Christ of revelation.

It is upon this Physics that Père Teilhard simultaneously builds up, secondly, a Mysticism:

The whole of Evolution being reduced to a process of union (communion) with God, it becomes, in its totality, loving and lovable in the innermost and most ultimate of its developments.

Taken together the three branches of the system (physics, apologetics and mysticism) suggest and readily lend themselves to forming an outline of a Metaphysics of Union, dominated by love, in which even the Problem of Evil is given an acceptable intellectual solution (the statistical necessity of disorders within a multitude in process of organization).

This 'philosophy' has been criticized as being no more than a generalized Concordism. To this Père Teilhard answers that concordism and coherence should not be confused. Religion and science obviously represent two different meridians on the mental sphere, and it would be wrong not to keep them separate (that is the concordist mistake); but these meridians must necessarily meet somewhere at a pole of common vision (that is, coherence). Otherwise all that is ours in the domain of thought and knowledge collapses.

New York, April, 1948

Epilogue

Autobiographical Evidence
1918–1934–1955

Prayer to the Ever-greater
Christ

1918. Extracts from *The Priest*

You have shown me the essential task of self-fulfilment in the plenitude of your incarnate Word, to which the world, through a chosen part of its *whole* being, is summoned ...

The Universality of your divine attraction, and the intrinsic value of our human activity – I am on fire, Lord, to make known to all this twofold truth you have revealed to me, and to make it real. ...

And I, Lord, for my (very lowly) part, would wish to be the apostle – and, if I dare be so bold – the evangelist – *of your Christ in the Universe.*

Through my thinking, through the message I bring, through the practical activity of my whole life, I would wish to disclose and make known to men the bonds of continuity that make the Cosmos of our restless ferment into an ambience that is divinized by the Incarnation, that divinizes by communion, and that is divinizable by our co-operation.

To bring Christ, by virtue of a specifically organic connection, to the heart of realities that are esteemed to be the most dangerous, the most unspiritual, the most pagan – in that you have my gospel and my mission.

If men could only see that in each one of them there is an element of the Pleroma, would not that, Lord, effect the reconciliation between God and our age? If only they could understand that, with all its natural richness and its massive reality, the universe can find fulfilment only in Christ; and that Christ, in turn, can be attained only through a universe that has been carried to the very limit of its capabilities.

To those who are seduced by the treasure-house of the

Real and overcome by its immediacy – to these I would show the life of the Lord Jesus flowing through all things – the true soul of the world.

To those who are dazzled by the nobility of human endeavour, I would say, in the name of Christ, that man's work is sacred, sacred both in the submission of the will to God, and in the great task it accomplishes in the course of endless tentative efforts – and that task is the liberation, natural and supernatural, of Spirit.

To those who are indolent, unenterprising, infantile, or narrow-minded in their religious attitude, I would point out that man's development is essential to Christ for the formation of his Body, and that a constant *spirit of inquiry* directed towards the world and truth *is an absolute duty.* . . .

Lord, to see drawn from so much wealth, lying idle or put to base uses, all the dynamism that is locked up within it: this is my dream. And to share in bringing this about: this is the work to which I would dedicate myself.

As far as my strength will allow me, *because I am a priest,* I would henceforth be the first to become aware of what the world loves, pursues, suffers. I would be the first to seek, to sympathize, to toil: the first in self-fulfilment, the first in self-denial – I would be more widely human in my sympathies and more nobly terrestrial in my ambitions than any of the world's servants.

On the one hand I want to plunge into the midst of created things and, mingling with them, seize hold upon and disengage from them all that they contain of life eternal, down to the very last fragment, so that nothing may be lost; and on the other hand I want, by practising the counsels of perfection, to salvage through self-denial all the heavenly fire imprisoned within the threefold concupiscence of the flesh, of avarice, of pride: in other words, to hallow, through chastity, poverty, and obedience, the power enclosed in love, in gold, in independence.

That is why I have taken on my vows and my priesthood (and it is this that gives me my strength and my happiness), in a determination to accept and divinize the powers of the earth. (W.T.W., pp. 206–22.)

In order that the Spirit may ever shine forth in me, that I may not succumb to the temptation that lies in wait for every act of boldness, nor ever forget that you alone must be sought in and through everything, I know, Lord, that you will send me – at what moments only you know – deprivations, disappointments, sorrow. The object of my love will fall away from me, or I shall outgrow it. (W.T.W., p. 126.)

1934. Extracts from *How I Believe*

The originality of my belief lies in its being rooted in two domains of life which are commonly regarded as antagonistic. By upbringing and intellectual training, I belong to the 'children of heaven'; but by temperament, and by my professional studies, I am a 'child of the earth'. Situated thus by life at the heart of two worlds with whose theory, idiom and feelings intimate experience has made me familiar, I have not erected any watertight bulkhead inside myself. On the contrary, I have allowed two apparently conflicting influences full freedom to react upon one another deep within me. And now, at the end of that operation, after thirty years devoted to the pursuit of interior unity, I have the feeling that a synthesis has been effected naturally between the two currents that claim my allegiance. The one has not destroyed, but has reinforced, the other. Today I believe probably more profoundly than ever in God, and certainly more than ever in the world. On an individual scale, may we not see in this the particular solution, at least in outline, of the great spiritual problem which the vanguard of mankind, as it advances, is now coming up against? . . .

For my own part, I set out resolutely in the only direction in which it seemed to me possible to carry my faith further, and so retain it. I tried to place at the head of the universe which I adored from birth, the risen Christ whom others had taught me to know. And the result of that attempt has been that I have never for the last twenty-five years ceased to marvel at the infinite possibilities which the 'universalization' of Christ opens up for religious thought. . . .

In truth, the more I have thought about the magnificent cosmic attributes lavished by St Paul on the risen Christ, and the more I have considered the masterful significance of the Christian virtues, the more clearly have I realized that Christianity takes on its full value only when extended (as I find it rewarding to do) to cosmic dimensions. Inexhaustibly fructified by one another, my individual faith in the world and my Christian faith in Christ have never ceased to develop and grow more profound. *By this sign*, which argues a continual agreement between what is most determinedly emergent in me and what is most alive in the Christian religion, I have finally and permanently recognized that in the latter I have found the complement I sought to my own self, and to that I have surrendered.

But, if I have thus surrendered myself, why should not others, all others, also do the same? . . .

The passion for the world from which my faith springs; the dissatisfaction, too, which I experience at first when I am confronted by any of the ancient forms of religion – are not both these traces in my heart of the uneasiness and expectancy which characterize the religious state of the world today? . . .

In that case, surely the solution for which modern mankind is seeking must essentially be exactly the solution which I have come upon. I believe that this is so, and it is in this vision that my hopes are fulfilled. A general convergence of religions upon a universal Christ who fundamentally satisfies them all: that seems to be the only possible conversion of the world, and the only form in which a religion of the future can be conceived. (*How I Believe*, pp. 7–8, 39, 40–1.)

1955. Extracts from *Le Christique*

Conclusion: The Promised Land

Energy becoming transformed into Presence.

And in consequence the possibility can be seen, opening up for man, of not only believing and hoping but (something much more unexpected and valuable) of loving, co-extensively and co-organically with the whole past, the present and the future of a Universe that is in process of concentrating upon itself. . . .

It would seem that a single ray of such a light falling like a spark, no matter where, on the Noosphere, would be bound to produce an explosion of such violence that it would almost instantaneously set the face of the earth ablaze and make it entirely new.

How is it, then, that as I look around me, still dazzled by what I have seen, I find that I am almost the only person of my kind, the only one to have seen? And so, I cannot, when asked, quote a single writer, a single work, that gives a clearly expressed description of the wonderful 'Diaphany' that has transfigured everything for me?

How, most of all, can it be that 'when I come down from the mountain' and in spite of the glorious vision I still retain, I find that I am so little a better man, so little at peace, so incapable of expressing in my actions, and thus adequately communicating to others, the wonderful unity that I feel encompassing me?

Is there in fact a Universal Christ, is there a divine Milieu?

Or am I, after all, simply the dupe of a mirage in my own mind?

I often ask myself that question.

Every time, however, that I begin to doubt, three successive waves of evidence rise up from deep within me to counter that doubt, sweeping away from my mind the mistaken fear that my 'Christic' may be no more than an illusion.

First there is the evidence provided by the *coherence* that this ineffable Element (or Milieu) introduces into the underlying depths of my mind and heart. As, of course, I know only too well, in spite of the ambitious grandeur of my ideas, I am still, in practice imperfect to a disturbing degree. For all the claims implicit in its expression, my faith does not produce in me as much real charity, as much calm trust, as the catechism still taught to children produces in the humble worshipper kneeling beside me. Nevertheless I know too that this sophisticated faith, of which I make such poor use, is the only faith I can tolerate, the only faith that can satisfy me – and even (of this I am certain) the only one that can meet the needs of the simple souls, the good folk, of tomorrow.

Next there is the evidence provided by the *contagious power* of a form of charity in which it becomes possible to love God 'not only with all one's body and all one's soul' but with the whole Universe-in-evolution. It would be impossible for me, as I admitted earlier, to quote a single 'authority' (religious or lay) of whom I could claim that in it I can fully recognize myself, whether in relation to my 'cosmic' or my 'Christic' vision. On the other hand, I cannot fail to feel around me – if only from the way in which 'my ideas' are becoming more widely accepted – the pulsation of countless people who are all – ranging from the border-line of unbelief to the depths of the cloister – thinking and feeling, or at least beginning vaguely to feel, just as I do. It is indeed heartening to know that I am not a lone discoverer but that I am, quite simply, responding to the vibration that (given a particular condition of Christianity and of the world) is necessarily active in all the souls around me. It is, in consequence, exhilarating to feel that I am not just myself or all alone, that my name is legion, that I am 'all men' and that this is true even in as much as the single-mindedness of to-morrow can be recognized as throbbing into life in the depths of my being.

Finally, there is the evidence contained in the *superiority* of my vision compared with what I had been taught – even though there is at the same time an *identity* with it. Because of their very function, neither the God who draws us to himself, nor the world whose evolution we share, can be a less powerful stimulant than we conceive and need. In either case – unless we are going to accept a positive discord in the very stuff of things – it is in the direction of the fullest that truth lies. Now, as we saw earlier, it is in the 'Christic' that, in the century in which we live, the Divine reaches the summit of adorability, and the evolutionary the extreme limit of activation. This can mean only one thing, that it is in that direction that the human must inevitably incline, there, sooner or later, to find unity.

Once that is realized, I immediately find a perfectly natural explanation for my isolation and apparent idiosyncrasy.

Everywhere on earth, at this moment, in the new spiritual atmosphere created by the idea of evolution, there float, in a state of extreme mutual sensitivity, love of God and faith in the world: the two essential components of the Ultra-human. These two components are everywhere 'in the air'; generally, however, they are not strong enough, *both at the same time*, to combine with one another *in one and the same subject*. In me, it happens by chance (temperament, upbringing, background) that the proportion of one to the other is correct, and the fusion of the two has been effected spontaneously – not as yet with sufficient force to spread explosively – but strong enough nevertheless to make it clear that the process is possible – and that *sooner or later there will be a chain-reaction*.

This is one more proof that the Truth has to appear only once, in one single mind, for it to be impossible for anything ever to prevent it from spreading universally and setting everything ablaze.

(Unpublished.)

Prayer to the Ever-greater Christ

Because, Lord, by every innate impulse and through all the hazards of my life I have been driven ceaselessly to search for you and to set you in the heart of the universe of matter, I shall have the joy, when death comes, of closing my eyes amidst the splendour of a universal transparency aglow with fire. . . .

It is as if the fact of bringing together and connecting the two poles, tangible and intangible, external and internal, of the world which bears us onwards had caused everything to burst into flames and set everything free.

In the guise of a tiny baby in its mother's arms, obeying the great laws of birth and infancy, you came, Lord Jesus, to swell in my infant soul; and then, as you re-enacted in me – and in so doing extended the range of – your growth through the Church, that same humanity which once was born and dwelt in Palestine began now to spread out gradually everywhere like an iridescence of unnumbered hues through which, without destroying anything, your presence penetrated – and endued with supervitality – every other presence about me.

And all this took place because, in a universe which was disclosing itself to me as structurally convergent you, by right of your resurrection, had assumed the dominating position of all-inclusive Centre in which everything is gathered together. (H.U., p. 150.)

As mankind emerges into consciousness of the movement that carries it along, it has a continually more urgent need of a Direction and a Solution ahead and above, to which it will at last be able to consecrate itself.

Who, then, is this God, no longer simply the God of the old Cosmos but the God of the new Cosmogenesis – so constituted precisely because the effect of a mystical operation that has been going on for two thousand years has been to disclose in you, beneath the Child of Bethlehem and the Crucified, the moving Principle and the all-embracing Nucleus of the World itself? Who is this God for whom our generation looks so eagerly? Who but you, Jesus, who represent him and bring him to us?

Lord of consistence and union, you whose *distinguishing mark* and *essence* is the power indefinitely to grow greater, without distortion or loss of continuity, to the measure of the mysterious Matter whose Heart you fill and all whose movements you ultimately control – Lord of my childhood and Lord of my last days – God, complete in relation to yourself and yet, for us, continually being born – God, who, because you offer yourself to our worship as 'evolver' and 'evolving', are henceforth the only being that can satisfy us – sweep away at last the clouds that still hide you – the clouds of hostile prejudice and those, too, of false creeds.

Let your universal Presence spring forth in a blaze that is, at once Diaphany and Fire.

O ever-greater Christ!

(From *Le Coeur de la Matière*, 1950, unpublished.)

Bibliography

Works by Teilhard de Chardin

1. The Phenomenon of Man (1938–40), English translation published by Collins, London, and Harper, New York, 1959, revised edition, 1965.

A scientific treatise setting out the phenomenology of evolution in the form of a law of recurrence, i.e. the law of complexity-consciousness.

Contents

Introduction by Sir Julian Huxley
Preface
Foreword: Seeing

Book One: Before Life Came

I.   The Stuff of the Universe
II. The Within of Things
III. The Earth in its Early Stages

Book Two: Life

I.   The Advent of Life
II. The Expansion of Life
III. Demeter

Book Three: Thought

I.   The Birth of Thought
II. The Deployment of the Noosphere
III. The Modern Earth

Let Me Explain

Book Four: Survival

2. The Appearance of Man, English translation published by Collins, London, and Harper & Row, New York, 1965. A collection of scientific articles on this subject.

Contents

3. The Vision of the Past. English translation published by Collins, London, and Harper & Row, New York, 1966. A collection of essays in science and the philosophy of science dealing with problems raised by Evolution and the phenomenon of man.

Contents

4. Le Milieu Divin (1926–7), English translation published by Collins, London, and Harper, New York (under the title *The Divine Milieu*), 1960.

A book of spirituality which at the same time gives an insight into Père Teilhard's own spiritual life. 'Le Milieu Divin', he wrote in 1934, 'is precisely my own self.'

Contents

Preface
Introduction

Part One: The Divinization of our Activities

1. The Christian Problem of the Sanctification of Action
2. An Incomplete Solution: Human Action Has no Value other than the Intention which Directs It.
3. The Final Solution: All Endeavour co-operates to complete the world in Christo Jesu
4. Communion Through Action
5. The Christian Perfection of Human Endeavour
6. Detachment Through Action.

Bibliography

Part Two: The Divinization of our Passivities

1. The Extent, Depth and Diverse Forms of Human Passivities
2. The Passivities of Growth and the Two Hands of God
3. The Passivities of Diminishment

Conclusion to the two first parts
Some General Remarks on Christian Ascetism

1. Attachment and Detachment
2. The Meaning of the Cross
3. The Spiritual Power of Matter

Part Three: The Divine Milieu

1. The Attributes of the Divine Milieu
2. The Nature of the Divine Milieu. The Universal Christ and the Great Communion
3. The Growth of the Divine Milieu

Epilogue
In Expectation of the Parousia

5. The Future of Man, English translation published by Collins, London, and Harper & Row, New York, 1964.
A collection of essays, concrete and closely reasoned, on the direction followed by Evolution after, in man, becoming conscious of itself.

Contents

6. Human Energy, English translation published by Collins, London, 1969.
In their method, these are the most fully worked-out of Teilhard's essays. They include valuable comments on morality and on love (sexual, human, and religious).

Bibliography

Contents

1. The Spirit of the Earth (1931)
2. The Significance and Positive Value of Suffering (1933)
3. Sketch of a Personalistic Universe (1936)
4. The Phenomenon of Spirituality (1937)
5. Human Energy (1937)
6. The Mysticism of Science (1939)

7. The Activation of Energy[1] (L'Activation de L'Énergie, Éditions du Seuil, Paris).
This deals more particularly with the universality, irreversibility, and unanimization demanded by human action.

Contents

1. The moment of choice (1939)
2. The Atomism of Spirit (1941)
3. The Rise of the Other (1942)
4. Universalization and Union (1942)
5. Centrology (1944)
6. The Analysis of Life (1945)
7. Outline of a Dialectic of Spirit (1946)
8. The Place of Technology in a General Biology of Mankind (1947)
9. On the Nature of the Phenomenon of Human Society (1948)
10. The Psychological Conditions of the Unification of Man (1949)
11. A Phenomenon of Counter-evolution, or the Existential Fear (1949)
12. The Sense of the Species in Man (1949)
13. The Evolution of Responsibility in the World (1950)
14. A Clarification (1950)
15. The Zest for Living (1951)

[1] English translation in preparation.

8. Man's Place in Nature (originally entitled *Le Groupe zoologique humain*) (1949), English translation published by Collins, London, and Harper & Row, New York, 1966.
A complete exposition, didactically presented, of Teilhard's phenomenology (biological evolution, the appearance of man, the development of human society), in which the treatment is more strictly scientific than in *The Phenomenon of Man*.

Contents

Introduction

I. The Place and Significance of Life in the Universe
A Self-Involuting World

1. Physics and Biology: the Problem

Let Me Explain

V. The Formation of the Noosphere

9. Science and Christ, English translation published by Collins, London, and Harper & Row, New York, 1968. Contains all the essays in which Père Teilhard set out to show the relation of Christianity and the fact of religion to Science and Society, and to indicate in what direction Christianity must make a deeper impact if it is to be the religion of tomorrow, 'the message for which the world is waiting'.

Contents

10. Comment je crois (How I believe), Éditions du Seuil, Paris.

Religious essays written between 1919 and 1953.

Contents

10. Christ the Evolver (8 October 1942)
11. Introduction to the Christian Life (29 June 1944)
12. Christianity and Evolution (11 November 1945)
13. Some Reflections on Original Sin (November 1947)
14. The Christian Phenomenon (10 May 1950)
15. Monogenism and Monophyletism (end 1950)
16. What the World awaits from the Church of God (14 September 1952)
17. The Contingence of the Universe and Man's Urge to Survive (1 May 1953)
18. A Sequel to the Problem of the Origin of Man, the Plurality of Inhabited Worlds (5 June 1953)
19. The God of Evolution (25 October 1953)
20. My Litanies (probably end 1953)

11. **Ma perspective du monde** (My View of the World – probable title), Éditions du Seuil, Paris.

12. **Le Coeur de la Matière** (The Heart of Matter), Éditions du Seuil, Paris (autobiographical papers).

13. **Hymn of the Universe**, English translation published by Collins, London, and Harper, New York, 1965. Religious and lyrical writings which express Père Teilhard's vivid awareness of God in all things, and of Christ as the focus of the world.

Contents

The Mass on the World
   Introduction by N. M. Wildiers, s.t.d.
   The Offering

Fire over the Earth
Communion
. Prayer

Christ in the World of Matter
The Picture
The Monstrance
The Pyx

The Spiritual Power of Matter
Hymn to Matter

Pensées *selected by Fernande Tardivel*
The Presence of God in the World
Humanity in Progress
The Meaning of Human Endeavour
In the Total Christ

14. Writings in Time of War, English translation published by Collins, London, and Harper & Row, New York, 1968.
A collection of essays written during the war of 1914–18, which Père Teilhard discussed in letters to his cousin (*The Making of a Mind*: see below).

Contents

1. Cosmic Life (1916)
2. Mastery of the World, and the Kingdom of God (1916)
3. The Struggle against the Multitude (1917)
4. The Mystical Milieu (1917)
5. Creative Union (1917)
6. The Soul of the World (1918)
7. The Eternal Feminine (1918)

8. The Priest (1918)
9. Operative Faith (1918)
10. Forma Christi (1918)
11. Note on the 'Universal Element' in the World (1918)
12. The Promised Land (1919)
13. The Universal Element (1919)

LETTERS

These are indispensable for an understanding of the inner evolution of Père Teilhard's thought. The style is most attractive and they make easy reading.

15. **Letters from Egypt** (1905–8), Éditions Aubier, Paris.
16. **Letters from Hastings and Paris** (1908–14), Éditions Aubier, Paris.
17. **The Making of a Mind, letters from a soldier-priest** (1914–18), English translation published by Collins, London, and Harper & Row, New York, 1965.
18. **Letters from a Traveller** (1923–55) (which includes the valuable *Teilhard: The Man*, by Pierre Leroy, s.j.), English translation published by Collins, London, and Harper & Row, New York, 1962.
19. **Letters to Léontine Zanta** (1923–39), English translation published by Collins, London, and Harper & Row, New York, 1969.

Suggestions for Further Study

For Teilhard's *method* (Chapter 1), see in particular:
  P. M., pp. 31–40
  H.E., pp. 19–24, 53–4, 113–14
  S.C., pp. 21–36

For *The Vision of the Past* and *The Phenomenon of Man*:
  P. M., pp. 43–57
  A.M., pp. 33–57, 132–65, 208–68
  V.P., pp. 51–79, 143–50, 161–233
  F.M., pp. 61–70, 97–120
  M.P.N., pp. 13–95
  S.C., pp. 86–97, 192–6

For *The Future of Man*
  P.M., pp. 261–78
  A.M., pp. 165–71, 244–70
  The whole of F.M.
  H.E., pp. 38–43, 61–5
  A.E., pp. 293–332
  M.P.N., pp. 79–121

For *Human Energy and its activation by Omega Point*:
  P.M., pp. 279–318
  A.M., pp. 244–70
  The whole of H.E.
  The whole of A.E., and in particular, pp. 83, 175, 237, 333, 379, 407, 417
  S.C., pp. 128–50

For Part 2 (Apologetics):
  P.M., pp. 319–27
  F.M., pp. 89–96

179

H.E., pp. 43–7, 89–92, 137–60
A.E., pp. 147–58
S.C., pp. 14–20, 98–112, 118–27, 187–91

For Part 3 (Morality and Mysticism):
H.E., pp. 145–55
The whole of M.D. and H.U.
S.C., pp. 199–205, 214–20

For a comprehensive view of Père Teilhard's thought, see:
P.M. (method, the phenomenon of man, the vision of the past, the future of man, apologetics)
Cosmic Life, in W.T.W., pp. 13–71
Creative Union, ibid., pp. 151–76
My Universe, in S.C., pp. 37–85
Super-humanity, Super-Christ, Super-Charity, ibid., pp. 151–73
Comment je vois, to be published in *Oeuvres* XII
Le Christique, to be published in *Oeuvres* XII

Index

Index

Also available in the Fontana Religious Series

The Prayer of the Universe
TEILHARD DE CHARDIN

A selection of Teilhard's most beautiful writings. This book will appeal to the thousands of readers who have read and re-read his best-sellers *Le Milieu Divin* and *Hymn of the Universe*.

To Me Personally
WILF WILKINSON

'When Wilf Wilkinson talks about the Bible, he makes it seem as though it has just been written, and not what some people think it is – 2,000 years out of date!'   *Roy Trevivian*

The Great Divorce
C. S. LEWIS

'It is all very witty, very entertaining, very readable, and Mr Lewis's fecundity of imagination is a thing to marvel at.'
Roger Lloyd, Time and Tide

The Difference in Being a Christian Today
JOHN A. T. ROBINSON

'Dr Robinson is addressing himself not to the rarefied world of *haute theologie* but to men of more modest academic pretensions or of none, which he does, nevertheless without talking down. . . . His is the theology of the people and for the people.'   *Clifford Longley, The Times*

Also available in the Fontana Religious Series

How Modern Should Theology Be?
HELMUT THIELICKE

'Thielicke touches on basic theological issues for today, but he does it with such a light hand, and with such graphic powers of illustration that I really cannot recall any other modern preacher who is so much *au fait* with modern theological questions.'
Ronald Gregor Smith

Strange Victory
GORDON W. IRESON

The Gospel, we are told, is Good News. What of? When we invite a man to become a Christian, what exactly are we offering to him, and asking him? These are some of the questions this book seeks to answer.

Companion to the Good News
JOSEPH RHYMER and ANTHONY BULLEN

More than 30 million people have bought *Good News for Modern Man* since it was first published. This 'Companion' has been written to help people understand the New Testament.

Apologia Pro Vita Sua
J. H. NEWMAN

A passionate defence of Cardinal Newman's own intellectual and spiritual integrity by a man who had been under continuous attack for many years.

Also available in the Fontana Religious Series

The Divine Pity
GERALD VANN

Undoubtedly Gerald Vann's masterpiece. Many people have insisted that this book should not merely be read, but re-read constantly, for it becomes more valuable the more it is pondered upon.

The Founder of Christianity
C. H. DODD

A portrait of Jesus by the front-ranking New Testament scholar. 'A first-rate and fascinating book . . . this book is a theological event.'   *Times Literary Supplement*

Science and Christian Belief
C. A. COULSON

'Professor Coulson's book is one of the most profound studies of the relationship of science and religion that has yet been published.'   *Times Literary Supplement*

Something Beautiful for God
MALCOLM MUGGERIDGE

'For me, Mother Teresa of Calcutta embodies Christian love in action. Her face shines with the love of Christ on which her whole life is centred. *Something Beautiful for God* is about her and the religious order she has instituted.'
Malcolm Muggeridge

Jesus Rediscovered
MALCOLM MUGGERIDGE

'. . . one of the most beautifully written, perverse, infuriating, enjoyable and moving books of the year.'
David L. Edwards, Church Times